IDIOMS IN USE

By Jacqueline Melvin

Introduction

The English language is rich in idiomatic expressions. Almost every time English people speak they use them.

So what are idioms?

Idioms are commonly used expressions that mean something other than the literal meanings of their individual words.

There are endless idiomatic expressions especially about the weather. This is probably due to the fact that in Britain, people talk a lot about the weather. When they make small talk for example, it is usually about what the weather is like, or what it was like, or what it is going to be like. This is because the weather is so changeable. One minute it may be sunny and the next rainy.

In this book you will learn over 300 of the most common idiomatic expressions used in everyday life along with bonus sections which include numerous fixed expressions, phrasal verbs and 101 similes, along with the most commonly used proverbs and their meanings. What's more, there is a glossary which gives you the meanings of the most commonly used phrasal verbs -which are repeatedly used throughout the book.

It is a good idea to try to understand those phrasal verbs by the context you find them in, but if you are in any doubt whatsoever, then just go to the glossary at the back of the book for clarification. Each phrasal verb is underlined with an asterisk in front of it.

<u>Example</u>: *<u>come on</u>

So what are fixed expressions?

Fixed expressions lie at the interface of grammar and lexicon. They are phrases which must be used as part of a sentence. Their word order is completely unchangeable and the words cannot be substituted by other words. They are ways of expressing ideas and concepts and they have very specific meanings and border on the edge of being idiomatic. Fixed phrases have a single meaning as though they are only one word.

How can I tell the difference between an idiom and a fixed phrase?

With an idiom you can usually express the same idea using other words. With a fixed phrase, you cannot.

What are similes?

Similes use figurative language to compare two things which are different. We use 'as' or 'like' with similes. The word 'simile' means 'similar to'.

Proverbs also play a large role in the English language. Proverbs are wise sayings used by people all the time, especially when giving advice.

GENERAL IDIOMS

A bag of bones

Meaning: When a person is so thin that they are all bones and no flesh.

Examples: If she doesn't start eating properly she'll *end up in hospital. She's **a bag of bones**.

When we found Sammy our dog he was **a bag of bones**. Someone had dumped him and it looked as if he hadn't eaten in weeks. Now he's a healthy dog and has *put on weight.

At the crack of dawn

Meaning: Daybreak; when night ends and morning begins.

Examples: I *get up every morning **at the crack of dawn**; just as the birds *wake up and start to chirp.

She is a very hard worker. She works from **the crack of dawn until dusk**.

At the drop of a hat

Meaning: To do something instantly without any hesitation/at a moment's notice.

Example: If you need any help, just phone me. I'll be there **at the drop of a hat**.

To be back to square one

<u>Meaning</u>: To be in the same position you were originally. To be no further forward/ to make an attempt that fails.

<u>Example</u>: I did a lot of overtime to get enough money to pay for my holiday. I saved for months and months and then I got a huge tax bill and all the money I had saved went on that. Now I **am back to square one**.

This idiomatic expression originates from board games such as monopoly. On the board game if you lose you go **back to square one** and begin all over again.

The ball is in your court

<u>Meaning</u>: When you are in a weak position and ∗<u>it is up to</u> someone else to make a decision as there is nothing else you can do.

<u>Example</u>: I've done everything possible to try to negotiate the deal with the manager of the company. He still hasn't given me a 'yes' or a 'no'. **The ball is in his court**.

Origin:

Metaphorical, this comes from tennis. When the ball is in your opponent's side of the net, he is the one to make the next move.

Be glad to see the back of something or someone

Meaning: To be happy and relieved not to see a certain person again.

Example: I can't wait to move house. I'll **be glad to see the back of my neighbour**. All she ever does is complain about everything.

To beat about the bush

Meaning: To avoid speaking directly about the main issue.

Example: **Don't beat about the bush**. Just get to the point and tell me what you did with all my money.

To beat the clock

Meaning: To manage to do something before a set time/a deadline.

Examples: We've only got a few hours left to finish this project. Let's see if we can **beat the clock**.

Luckily we managed **to beat the clock** and get to the airport just as the check in desk was closing.

A similar expression is:

A race against time

Example: It was **a race against time** for the taxi driver to get us to the airport.

A blessing in disguise

Meaning: Something good which you thought was really bad at the time it happened.

Example: I was in a terrible state when I lost my job. It *turned out to be **a** real **blessing in disguise** because I now run my own business. If I hadn't lost my job I would still be working ten hours a day for a paltry salary. Now I am earning megabucks.

To be a chip off the old block

Meaning: To be the same as your father.

Example: He has a real passion for photography. He**'s a** real **chip off the old block**. His father has this passion too.

To chip in

Meaning: This means to contribute some money to buy something for someone.

Example: It's Sally's birthday next week. Why don't we all **chip in** and get her a nice gift?

To cut a long story short

Meaning: To tell someone the main point without giving all the details.

Example: I don't have time at the moment to tell you everything that happened to me on the way home last night but **to cut a long story short** we had to abandon the car and get a taxi. I'll tell you everything this evening.

To be a far cry from

Meaning: To be very different from.

Example: It's great living in my new house. Everything is new and we have a beautiful garden. It**'s a far cry from** the last one. It was old and had no garden.

Down to earth

Meaning: A person who is not pretentious and is easy to *get on with; of simple style and manner. (Used as an adjective form with the verb 'be')

Example: Even though he is rich and famous, he has never let it go to his head. He is a very **down to earth** guy.

Get a grip

Meaning: To control your emotions.

Example: You've been crying endlessly for days after losing your job. It's time to **get a grip** and start looking for a new one.

Get your skates on

Meaning: This is used to tell people to *hurry up.

Example: **Get your skates on** or we'll miss the train.

To get out of bed on the wrong side

Meaning: When a person is irritated and grumpy, we use this idiom

Example: It's better not to speak to the boss just yet. He's in a terrible mood. He's been annoyed since the moment he got here. I think he must have **got out of bed on the wrong side** this morning.

Hard to come by

Meaning: This means that something is difficult to find.

Example: Nowadays it's **hard to come by** those little old electrical repair shops that there used to be in every area.

Has/Have got it made

Meaning: To have the perfect life -we use the subject before 'has/have' to indicate 'who's' got it made'.

Example: She**'s got it made** in that job. She earns a fortune but does nothing all day.

Let bygones be bygones

Meaning: To forget about past problems or disputes you had with someone.

Example: Person A: "I'll never forget how badly I treated you. Can you ever forgive me?"

Person B: "**Let bygones be bygones**".

Another idiom with the same meaning is:

It's all water under the bridge.

To be at your wit's end

Meaning: This means to be extremely worried and upset. You are so worried that you feel you will go crazy.

Example: Mother to son: Where have you been all night? I've **been at my wit's end** with worry.

To be in (someone's) bad books

Meaning: This means someone is not happy with you because you did something they didn't like or because you didn't do something you were supposed to do.

Example: I**'m in my father's bad books** again for using his car without his permission. I thought he would never *find out but he did.

To be in hot water

Meaning: To be in a bad situation/ to be in terrible trouble

Example: I'll most definitely **be in hot water** when dad *finds out I crashed his car. I think I'd better try to get a hold of a mechanic to repair the damage before he *finds out.

To be the living proof of something

Meaning: This means that you exemplify something. Your experience of something shows that this can happen.

Example: You can do anything you want to do. You can be anything you want to be. I **am the living proof of that**. Do not be afraid to follow your dream and never *give up.

Mum's the word

Meaning: This means that you have promised not to tell anyone someone's secret.

Example: "Can you keep a secret?" "**Mum's the word**" (I promise not to breathe a word to anyone).

To jump on the bandwagon

Meaning: To do what everyone else is doing because it is a popular thing to do and because it is beneficial to you/follow the current trend.

Example: Many British companies have **jumped on the bandwagon** and transferred their call centres to India, saving thousands of pounds on salaries, and leaving thousands of Brits without a job. The trend is rising by the day.

Pull the wool over a person's eyes

Meaning: To deceive someone

Example: He thinks he can **pull the wool over my eyes** with his lies. Does he really think I am so stupid as to believe him?

To reach the end of (one's) tether

Meaning: When you can no longer *put up with a situation or person.

Example: I've **reached the end of my tether** with my teenage son. He does whatever he wants and nowadays he doesn't even speak to me anymore. He goes straight to his room, locks the door and stays there all evening. I'm *fed up trying to communicate with him. It is all just a waste of time.

Origin of this idiomatic expression:

A tether is a rope which is used to limit the movement of an animal. When you reach the end of your tether, you have reached the limit of your patience and feel so frustrated that you may just *give up trying.

Rub it in

Meaning: This idiom is used when someone keeps reminding another person of something he/she did wrong or some kind of failure in his/her life which is likely to cause embarrassment. Usually the person wishes to forget the whole episode. This expression can also be used playfully as you can see in the second example.

Example: I know I *fell off the chair at the meeting but do you have to keep **rubbing it in**?

Will you stop **rubbing it in** about your big win on the lottery?

To skate on thin ice

Meaning: This means that you put yourself in a risky dangerous situation. Just as in the literal meaning; if you skate on thin ice, you take the risk of the ice *giving way below your feet and you falling into the freezing water and possibly dying.

Examples: Do you go through life always **skating on thin ice** or do you keep to where the ground is solid and safe?

Every time he *gets on that motorbike and zooms off at top speed without wearing his helmet, he is **skating on thin ice**.

To sleep on it

Meaning: This means that you will reach a decision on a matter once you have carefully *thought it through. Have a good night's sleep and decide what to do the next day.

Example: Don't sign the contract just yet. It's better to **sleep on it**.

To be spoilt for choice

Meaning: This means when you have so much choice of something in front of you that you do not know what to choose.

Example: That new supermarket has about one hundred different types of shampoo. I **was** really **spoilt for choice today**. I just didn't know which brand to choose.

To be sick and tired of something or someone

Meaning: This means that you are just so*fed up. You find it difficult to tolerate something or something which is making you feel tired and unhappy.

Examples: I**'m sick and tired of** working all day every day. I need a break. A nice relaxing holiday would do me the world of good.

Mother to son: I**'m sick and tired of** telling you to stop leaving your wet bathrobe on the bathroom floor.

Take a hike

Meaning: When you are angry with someone and you want them to go away, you say: Go take a hike or take a hike.

Example: I don't believe a word you say. I don't want to hear any more of your lies and excuses. **Go take a hike** and *leave me alone. I've had enough of you.

To think outside the box

Meaning: To think differently/have an original idea/have the ability to conceive and evolve different approaches.

Example: We are looking for a new manager who can **think outside the box**. We need someone who can *come up with new ideas and new approaches.

To tread water

Meaning: To make very slow progress or no progress at all.

Example: As a society, I feel we have been **treading water** for too long. If we don't all start to work together to recover from this year's losses, I'm afraid we could *end up going bankrupt.

ANGER IDIOMS

To go bananas

Meaning: To get angry or excited or become crazy.

Example: He **went bananas** when I told him there was a scratch on his new car. You'd have thought it was my fault it was scratched by the way he reacted.

To flip the lid

Meaning: To go crazy or get angry (the same as 'to go bananas').

Example: My wife **flipped the lid** when she *found out I had another woman. She packed her bags and went back to her mother's soon after.

To flip it

Meaning: The same as 'to flip the lid' and 'go bananas'.

Example: His father **flipped it** when he *found out his son had been *playing truant. Seemingly it had been *going on for months on end.

*To play truant = not go to school when you are supposed to.

To hit the roof

Meaning: To get really angry.

Example: She **hit the roof** when she found out her son had been expelled from school.

To freak out

Meaning: To go crazy, get really angry (a stronger anger than 'to hit the roof').

Example: She **freaked out** when she saw how much the phone bill was.

To blow your top

Meaning: To get really angry

Example: My mother **blew her top** when she saw the mess we had made of the kitchen.

To jump down (someone's) throat

Meaning: To answer really badly when someone asks you something.

Example: You can't say a word to my brother these days or he **jumps down your throat** for the least little thing. Yesterday I asked him to pass me the remote control and once again he jumped down my throat screaming "I'm not your servant." I don't know what has *come over him lately.

To get on someone's nerves

Meaning: When someone does something that is irritating or bothering you.

Examples: Will you stop whistling! You're **getting on my nerves**.

My neighbours' children are playing in the garden and they're really **getting on my nerves** with their shouting and screaming.

To make your blood boil

Meaning: When someone does something that really annoys you.

Example: It really **makes my blood boil** when people are driving and speaking on their mobile phones. This behaviour could cause an accident.

To knock (someone's) socks off

Meaning: Used a lot by mothers who are not too happy when their child misbehaves. In this context it means I'll beat you so hard that your socks will come off. The mothers don't mean it. They just say it as an expression to show they are not happy. Nowadays it has a second meaning - to leave someone speechless when you do something very surprising.

Examples: Mother to son: If you don't tidy your room **I'll knock your socks off.**

He really **knocked my socks off** by asking me to marry him in front of two hundred people.

To scream blue murder

Meaning: Used to express how a person screams when they are upset or angry. They scream so much that they are blue in the face. It also means that you complain a lot because you want to make yourself be noticed and heard.

Examples: She was **screaming blue murder** when she heard her husband had *gambled away all their savings.

When our baby needs his nappy changed, he **screams blue murder** until we change it.

The residents of the village have been **screaming blue murder**, at the mayor, for months. They want him to reopen the road that he authorized to close.

Animal Idioms

To be a black sheep

Meaning: To be the bad member of the family - completely different from all the other family members - usually in a negative sense.

Example: My son Tom is always in trouble with the police. He's the **black sheep** of the family.

Let the cat out of the bag

Meaning: This means 'to reveal a secret'.

Example: I'm getting engaged soon but it is secret for now. Please **don't let the cat out of the bag**. Don't let anyone know.

The cat is out of the bag

Meaning: Something is no longer a secret. The secret has been revealed.

Example: **The cat is out of the bag**. Everyone knows so there is no point in keeping it a secret anymore.

Spring chicken

Meaning: When we want to say that a woman is not young anymore, we say: "**She's no spring chicken**."

Example: Susan should think about *settling down. After all she is **no spring chicken** anymore. She's nearing her fifties.

To chicken out of something

Meaning: Not to *go through with a plan because of fear.

Example: He was going to *ask the girl out for dinner, but at the last moment he **chickened out**.

To see a man about a dog

Meaning: When you don't want anybody to know where you are going and you invent an excuse so as not to let them know what you are really going to do.

Example: "Where are you going?" "I'm going to **see a man about a dog**."

To think you are the bees' knees

Meaning: This means that you are vain; full of yourself.

Example: He really **thinks he's the bee's knees**. He thinks every girl that looks at him is in love with him.

To have a bee in your bonnet

Meaning: This means you are very irritated and you get angry if anyone tries to speak to you.

Example: I don't know what is wrong with Sally today. She must have **a bee in her bonnet**. I asked her for a loan of her pen and she *snapped at me.

A cat nap

Meaning: To *lie down and have a short rest or a short sleep. This idiom comes from the fact that cats have many naps and rest or sleep for short periods.

Example: After lunch: "I'm tired. I'm going to have **a cat nap**."

A little bird told me

Meaning: When we tell someone something we know about someone or something but we don't want to say who told us, we say: "**A little bird told me**."

Example: "How did you know I was getting married?" "**A little bird told me**."

Let sleeping dogs lie

Meaning: To leave things as they are so as to avoid causing any trouble. Just as in the literal sense, it is better not to disturb a dog that is sleeping as it may bite you.

Example: "We'll discuss the problem later. Your father is very angry at the moment so it is better to **let sleeping dogs lie**."

There's not enough room to swing a cat

Meaning: When a room or a house is very small, we say: "There's not enough room in here to swing a cat."

Example: "We can't have the party at my house because **there is not enough room to swing a cat**. I live in a tiny one room flat."

While the cat's away, the mouse will play

Meaning: People will do what they want when they are left unsupervised - especially in disregarding rules

Example: As soon as their parents left for their holidays, the teenagers had a wild party. **While the cat's away the mouse will play**.

The cat's whiskers

Meaning: This means that you think you are better than anyone else.

Example: He really thought he was **the cat's whiskers** as he was cruising along the road in his new car.

This has a very similar meaning to: 'He thinks he's the bees' knees'.

To go to the dogs

Meaning: To deteriorate or become bad.

Example: Since Italy converted to the euro, it has been slowly **going to the dogs**.

To be as sick as a dog

Meaning: This is used when you are really sick indeed.

Example: I **was as sick as a dog** all weekend. I had to stay in bed. I couldn't *get up and I completely lost my appetite.

I felt **as sick as a dog** when I heard the news. (When used with 'feel', it means you have a terrible feeling inside you).

To be dog tired

Meaning: This expression is used when you are so tired you have difficulty in keeping your eyes open.

Example: I had to go to bed as soon as I got home last night. I **was dog tired**. I didn't even have the energy to cook.

To smell a rat

Meaning: We use this idiom to indicate that we are suspicious about something.

Example: There's something not quite right with the balance sheet. **I smell a rat**.

To have ants in your pants

Meaning: When you are agitated about something or excited and you cannot keep still. You are always moving. If you really had ants in your pants, in the literal sense, you would not be able to sit down.

Example: You've got **ants in your pants**. What's wrong with you? You've been pacing up and down all morning.

It sounds fishy

Meaning: We use this expression when something seems very suspicious.

Example: The price of this car is far too low. We'd better *find out why. **It sounds fishy to me**.

We can also say: 'There's something fishy *going on.' This means that something suspicious is happening.

It's fishy business

This means the same. Something is not quite right. We suspect something.

To be a night owl

Meaning: This is used to describe person who likes doing things until very late in the evening - usually into the early hours of the morning instead of going to bed

Example: He**'s a real night owl**, but he can't *get up in the morning.

To be an early bird

Meaning: This is the opposite of a night owl. It refers to a person who is up bright and early in the morning.

Example: She**'s an early bird**. She's up every morning at 5.30.

The early bird catches the worm

Meaning: This means that if you are up early in the morning, you have more time to work and make money. If you stay in bed half the day, you will fall into poverty.

To have butterflies in your stomach

Meaning: When you have butterflies in your stomach, you feel very nervous or excited about something.

Examples: She **had butterflies in her stomach** when she was going to meet the boy she was in love with.

He **had butterflies in his stomach** the day he went for the job interview.

Talk until the cows come home

Meaning: Talk for a very long time without solving the problem or convincing a person to do something.

Examples: We can **talk until the cows come home** but we are never going to find a solution.

Mother to son: "I'm not going to buy you that new bike. You **can talk to me until the cows come home**. I'm not going to change my mind."

BODY IDIOMS

"I drink to separate my body from my soul."

— Oscar Wilde

To cost an arm and a leg

<u>Meaning</u>: When we say that something cost an arm and a leg, it means it was very expensive.

<u>Example</u>: My new car has **cost me an arm and a leg**. I've no idea how I am going to manage to *<u>pay off</u> these hefty monthly instalments. I'll have to find a second job.

To pay through the nose for something

<u>Meaning</u>: To pay a huge amount of money for something - the same meaning as 'to cost an arm and a leg'.

An eye for an eye and a tooth for a tooth

<u>Meaning</u>: This expression is used when someone does you a wrong and you *<u>pay</u> them <u>back</u> in the same way. We can also say -"Give someone a taste of his/her own medicine".

<u>Example</u>: He *<u>ripped me off</u> so now I am going to find a way to rip *him* off **good style. As the saying goes, '**an eye for an eye and a tooth for a tooth**.

**Good style implies 'in a very big way'.

To see eye to eye

Meaning: This means to agree with someone. It is used very often in the negative, that is, to disagree with someone.

Example: My boyfriend and I have *broken up because we didn't **see eye to eye**. (We didn't agree on anything)

To foot the bill

Meaning: Who is going to pay the bill? Who is going to **foot the bill**?

Example: She *ran up a huge phone bill and left her father **to foot the bill**.

Hit the nail on the head

Meaning: You really hit the nail right on the head = you understood perfectly well what I meant/ you got the precise point.

Example: He hit **the nail on the head** when he said Jane was only *going out with him for his money.

Scratch someone's back

Meaning: Do someone a favour if they will return it.

Example: You **scratch my back** and I will scratch yours = you do me a favour and I will return the favour.

Like music to my ear

Meaning: When someone says "it was **like music to my ears**," it means that it is exactly what you wanted to hear.

Example: When he told me he loved me, it was **like music to my ears**.

Play it by ear

Meaning: To deal with a situation as it develops.

Example: "The weather forecast says there may be a storm tomorrow so we might not be able to go out on the boat."

"Let's wait and see what happens. We'll just **play it by ear**."

To be all ears

Meaning: This means, 'don't worry, I'm paying attention to what you are saying.'

Examples: Boy to Mother: "You are not listening to me, are you?" Mother to boy: "Yes, of course I am. **I'm all ears**."

Girl to friend: "I've got some really exciting news to tell you." Friend to girl: "Great, tell me all about it, **I'm all ears**."

Two heads are better than one

Meaning: This means that if two people are working on a problem, they stand a better chance of finding a solution than if only one person was to work on it.

Example: Two of the company's top executives discussed why their contrasting strengths have created the perfect business relationship. Each of them has a different perception to any problem which may arise so they complement each other. They firmly believe that **two heads are better than one**.

Keep your eyes peeled

Meaning: To closely *watch out for someone or something.

Example: Man to neighbour: "My cat has disappeared. You don't happen to have seen it?" Neighbour to man: "No I haven't seen it but I will **keep my eyes peeled** while I'm out with my dog this afternoon. I'm sure it'll *turn up sooner or later.

To break your back

Meaning: To work extremely hard.

Example: I'm up every morning at the crack of dawn just as the night becomes day and home again late at night. I'm really **breaking my back** to pay all these bills.

Out of the goodness of (one's) heart

Meaning: If you do something out of the goodness of your heart, you do it as a kind act towards someone else. You have no wish to benefit from it, and you do not do it out of duty

Example: A:"I'll pay your mother for cleaning my house while I was ill in bed."B: "There's no need to pay her. She did it **out of the goodness of her heart**. She's very happy to help people."

To be back on your feet

Meaning: If you are back on your feet, after being ill, you are healthy again. We can also use this for a business if it is going badly and then things get better.

Examples: "Have you got over that bad flu you had?" "Yes, I've **been back on my feet** now for a few days."

The company almost had to *close down after *going through a bad period. Thanks to that big order that came in we are slowly getting **back on our feet again**.

To take something at face value

Meaning: Accept by appearance instead of going deeper into something.

Example: When I was younger and you went for a job interview, the employer hired you **at face value**. (He trusted you by your appearance and the way you spoke and presented yourself) Nowadays you have to go through psychology tests for some jobs and produce endless qualifications before you are even accepted for an interview.

To be written all over your face

Meaning: This means that it is very clear by your expression that you have done something. Usually it refers to guilt.

Example: It was definitely John who stole the money. Even though he denied it, it **was written all over his face**.

It's no skin off my nose

Meaning: This means that you are unaffected by a situation - it makes no difference to you.

Example: Person A: "Sorry you didn't get that job you went for". Person B: "**It's no skin off my nose**. I didn't want it anyway."

To be a pain in the neck

Meaning: No, it is not what you think it is. This doesn't mean that your neck hurts. We use this idiom to describe a very annoying person.

Example: She**'s** a real **pain in the neck**. She's always borrowing my things and she never gives me them back. I'm going to have to stop lending her my things.

To be on the tip of (one's) tongue

Meaning: We use this expression when we are about to say something but as the words are about to come out our mouths, we can't remember them. We become frustrated in that moment because we knew what we were going to say but in one second it disappears from our memory. We try desperately to remember.

Examples: What's the name of that new shop round the corner? I know the name - I've been there three times this week. Just a second, it**'s on the tip of my tongue**.

Oh gosh!!!!! I don't remember what this is called in English. I have always known. Give me a second or two and I'll remember. It**'s on the tip of my tongue**.

To bite (one's) tongue

Meaning: This doesn't mean that you are going to hurt yourself by biting your tongue with your teeth. It means that you refrain from saying what you really want to say, probably because it could cause some trouble.

Example: I always have **to bite my tongue** when my mother in law tells me in continuation that I'm not suitable for her son.

To keep someone at arm's length

Meaning: If you keep a person at arm's length then you avoid any familiarity with them. You do allow yourself to have any close contact with the person. There may be several reasons for this. Maybe you don't like the person or maybe you know this person could hurt you emotionally. You keep your distance from the person. Maybe the person is in love with you and you do not have any feelings for him/her and you do not wish to hurt them by allowing them to get too close to you.

Examples: The new boss **keeps us all at arm's length**. The last one was much friendlier and much more approachable.

I'm **keeping my ex boyfriend at arm's length**. I do not wish to get involved with him again. He keeps phoning but I rarely answer the phone whenever he rings me.

Colour Idioms

To have green fingers

Meaning: To be very good at gardening.

Example: My husband **has green fingers**. All our plants are *coming on really well.

A bolt from the blue

Meaning: When something happens very unexpectedly.

Example: It was like **a bolt from the blue** to find out that he had been lying to me for so long. I trusted him so much.

Out of the blue

Meaning: To appear suddenly or happen suddenly without any warning.

Example: I received a phone call **out of the blue** from my cousin in New York who I hadn't heard from in years.

Once in a blue moon

Meaning: Extremely rarely/almost never.

Example: Scotland has an *Indian summer **once in a blue moon**.

*See 'weather idioms'

To be off colour

Meaning: When you do not look very well. Your face is pale.

Examples: I'm taking my son to the doctor. He has **been off colour** for the past two days.

Our next door neighbour **was** a bit **off colour** this morning when I saw him. I wonder what's wrong with him.

To be in the red

Meaning: To have debt with the bank.

Example: I will have to *pay off my credit card debt. I**'m in the red**.

To be out of the red

Meaning: To have paid off all your debts.

Example: Thank God, that's all my debt *paid off. Now that I **am out of the red** I can relax.

To be green with envy

Meaning: We use this expression to say that someone is envious of another person or his/her belongings -the envy is so obvious it shows on the person's face.

Example: She **was green with envy** when she saw our new villa.

Red tape

Meaning: Official rules and bureaucratic paperwork.

Example: There's too much **red tape** to get a work permit for Australia.

The black market

Meaning: We usually say, 'buy something on the black market'. This means you bought something illegally such as stolen goods. We can also say: "I got it on the black market."

Example: "Where did you get that Rolex watch you're wearing? It must have cost you an arm and a leg." "Well actually I got it really cheap on **the black market**."

CRAZY MAD IDIOMS

"Show me a sane man and I will cure him for you".

To drive someone crazy/mad

Meaning: To irritate, annoy, upset or make someone lose patience.

Examples: He always floods the bathroom floor after having a shower. It's **driving me crazy** (the situation).

This new computer software is **driving me crazy**. I've been trying to *work out how to use it but I still haven't understood.

Mother to son: "Will you *turn that music down? It's **driving me mad**."

To drive like crazy

Meaning: Drive your car or other vehicle very fast and often dangerously.

Examples: He **drove like crazy** to get us to the airport in time. Luckily we didn't have an accident and managed to catch the flight.

I'm never ever going to get into John's car. He **drives like crazy**. He's a danger to himself and everyone on the road. I risked my life the last time he gave me a lift.

Like crazy

Meaning: A lot

Example: The tomatoes have grown **like crazy** this year. We've got enough to last us a life time.

To be crazy for someone

Meaning: To be in love or infatuated with someone.

Example: She**'s crazy for that new pop singer**.

To be mad at someone

Meaning: To be angry with

Examples: She **was mad at her son** for taking her car without her permission and to make matters worse, he wrecked it.

I**'m** really **mad at** my husband for forgetting my birthday.

To be mad about someone

Meaning: Like or love a lot.

Example: My daughter never studies anymore. All she does is *mope around all day thinking about that new boy in her class. She **is mad about him**. When I think about it, when I was her age I was **mad about** a boy in my class as well. As the saying goes, like mother, like daughter.

To be in a mad rush

Meaning: To run around chaotically in a terrible hurry.

Examples: I left my Christmas shopping to the last moment and ended up **being in a mad rush** to buy everything on Christmas Eve. Never again!

I'm always **in a mad rush** first thing in the morning. I'll need to try to get up earlier in the morning so I can take things easy.

To be stark raving mad

Meaning: To be absolutely crazy.

Examples: He **is stark raving mad** if he thinks I will work overtime without being paid.

She must **be stark raving mad** to have turned down that incredible job offer. Had it been me I would have jumped at the chance.

FOOD IDIOMS

"Bread that comes out of sweat, tastes better"

~ Italian proverb

To be full of beans

Meaning: No, it is not what you think it is. It does not mean you have eaten too many beans and now your body is full of them. It means 'to be super excited and lively, full of energy and in very high spirits'.

Example: She **was full of beans** this morning. She must be in love.

To spill the beans

Meaning: To reveal a secret.

Example: I've organised a surprise party for my parents' golden wedding anniversary but please don't **spill the beans**. They mustn't *find out about it.

It's a piece of cake

Meaning: No we don't mean that there is a nice piece of cake sitting in front of us waiting to be eaten. When we say something is a 'piece of cake,' it means it is extremely easy.

Example: "How did your exam go?" "It **was a piece of cake**." (I knew I was going to pass it as it was a really easy subject that I like very much).

It's not my cup of tea

Meaning: No, this does not mean that the cup of tea belongs to someone else and not you. The meaning of this idiom is: It is not my taste, it doesn't interest me. I don't really like this.

Example: Some people love watching sport on TV, but **it's not my cup of tea**. I prefer to go out and do sport than to watch it.

It's no use crying over spilt milk

Meaning: To complain about or get upset over something that happened and cannot be changed -a situation that is irreversible.

Example: Okay your girlfriend left you because of your bad behaviour. **It's no use crying over spilt milk**. What's done is done and she is never going to *come back. You will just have to get on with your life and learn from your mistakes.

To be packed together like sardines

Meaning: To be tightly packed in/squashed together.

Examples: We **were all packed together like sardines** on the bus coming home tonight. It was a nightmare, to say the least. I could hardly move or breathe. Never again! Next time I'm going to get a taxi.

I can't get anything else into my suitcase. Everything **is packed in like sardines**.

A couch potato

Meaning: This refers to a lazy person who usually lies on the couch all day watching TV.

Example: I've had enough of my son. He just lies there on the couch switching channels from morning to night. He has become **a real couch potato**. I've told him time and time again to get out there and look for a job.

To butter someone up

Meaning: This refers to a person who is really nice to you only to obtain something from you - to flatter. Flattery is a negative form of praise.

Example: He tried **to butter me up** but I didn't *fall for it. I knew he just wanted to borrow my new car.

To sell like hot cakes

Meaning: To be bought by many people.

Example: The new I-pad has really been **selling like hot cakes**. There are none left in the store. We'll have to re-order them.

To be cheesed off

Meaning: To be tired and *fed up with someone or something.

Example: I'**m really cheesed off** today. I was expecting to get that job but they *turned me down.

The cream of the crop

Meaning: Only the best

Example: The Company is hiring new managers but they will be doing a careful selection. They only want **the cream of the crop**.

A big cheese

Meaning: No, it doesn't mean a big piece of cheese. This refers to an influential person in a top position.

Example: **The big cheese** wants to have a word with you. He wants to know how things are progressing in our department.

A tough cookie

Meaning: In the literal sense this means a biscuit which is hard to bite but idiomatically it has another meaning; a tough cookie is a very determined person.

Example: He's **a real tough cookie**. It is difficult to *get through to him.

The apple of (one's) eye

Meaning: Someone you are really *fond of is the apple of your eye.

Example: My little daughter **is the apple of her daddy's eye**. He adores her.

Where did this phrase originate from? Well in old English, the phrase referred to the pupil of the eye, considered to be a globular solid body; it came to be used as a symbol of something cherished and *<u>watched over</u>.

HAPPINESS IDIOMS

The following idioms all have more or less the same meaning.

To be in seventh heaven

Meaning: To have a feeling of immense happiness

Example: She **was in seventh heaven** the day her baby was born.

To be on cloud nine

Meaning: To have an elated feeling of happiness

Example: She **was on cloud nine** when her husband bought her a diamond ring.

To be tickled pink

Meaning: To be feeling very pleased

Example: The baby**'s tickled pink** with its new teddy bear.

To be walking on air

Meaning: Used in the same way as 'to be on cloud nine'

To be on top of the world

Meaning: The same as the above idioms.

HOME IDIOMS

"Home is where the heart is".

To make yourself at home

Meaning: What you say to a guest to make him or her feel comfortable and relaxed.

Example: Man to friend: "If you want anything to eat while I am out, just open the fridge and eat what you want. There is no need to ask me. Just **make yourself at home**."

To be homesick

Meaning: This means to feel the absence of your own home. Some college students may miss their family and feel homesick.

Example: Whenever I **am homesick** I call my mother and father. Just hearing their voices makes me feel much better.

To move house

Meaning: To leave your current house and go to live in another one.

Example: I'**m moving house** next week. I've found a bigger place that costs less than this one. I can't wait to have more space to move around.

To move in

Meaning: To begin living in your new house. (This is a phrasal verb)

Example: "When are you **moving in** to your bigger place?" "If all goes well I should have the keys by next Monday."

To move out

Meaning: The opposite of 'move in'. (This, too is a phrasal verb)

Example: "I hope to **move out** on Monday morning and move in to my new place on the same day."

INTELLIGENCE IDIOMS

A smart cookie

Meaning: This refers to a very clever person -one who is a quick thinker.

Example: My boyfriend is **a real smart cookie**. He is a real whizz kid at computer programming.

A bright spark

Meaning: A person who is very clever and understands things easily and quickly

Example: My son is **a real bright spark**. He's only six and he can already read and write.

On the ball

Meaning: To always be active, attentive and aware of what is *going on.

Examples: He's really **on the ball** since he started eating healthily.

I have to go to bed early as I need to be **on the ball** all day in my job.

LOVE IDIOMS

"Immature love says: "I love you because I need you. Mature love says: I need you because I love you."

To be head over heels

Meaning: This means that you are madly in love with someone.

Example: Girl to her friend: "You look very happy today." Friend: "Yes, that is because I am very happy. I met a boy at a party last night and I**'m already head over heels**."

To pop the question

Meaning: Ask someone to marry you.

Example: At long last he has **popped the question**; I thought he would never ask.

To fall for someone

Meaning: To be strongly attracted to someone, possibly be infatuated by someone.

Example: She's really **fallen for** that new actor on TV. Her room is covered in posters of him. (Phrasal verb)

To get hitched

Meaning: To get married.

Example: He's finally going to **get hitched** after years of *putting it off.

MADNESS - INSANITY IDIOMS

"No great genius has ever existed without some touch of madness".

~Aristotle

When you think that someone is crazy- insane or eccentric, you can use the following idiomatic expressions to describe them:

To be not all there

<u>Example</u>: He walks around talking to himself all day. He's not all there.

All the following idiomatic expressions can be used in the same way:

He's got a screw loose.

He's dotty.

He's on another planet.

He's out of his mind. This can have two meanings, either he is crazy or he is drunk.

He's bonkers.

He's off his flipper.

He's off his rocker.

He's demented.

He's nutty.

He's a loony bin.

He's crackers.

He's off the wall.

He's lost his marbles.

He's a nutcase.

He's balmy.

He's nuts.

He's wacky.

He's not living in the real world.

He's spaced out. Triple Meaning: he's insane, he's drunk or he has taken drugs.

Money Idioms

Let's go Dutch

Meaning: Share the bill. If you are in a pub for example, you can either offer to pay for the drinks or you can say, '**let's go Dutch**'. 50/50

Nest egg

Meaning: When you have a '**nest egg**', it means you have put money aside for emergencies or you can inherit money and this can be called a 'nest egg'. A 'nest egg' is usually a substantial amount of money. If is it is not a lot of money, then we say: 'I've got a small nest egg put aside' just in case an unexpected expense *crops up.

Examples: I've got a **nest egg** to *fall back on when I retire.

John inherited a small **nest egg** when his aunt died.

A golden handshake

Meaning: It doesn't mean that someone with a golden hand is going to shake your hand. It is a payment paid to an employee when he leaves the company or if he takes early retirement. This payment is seen as a token of thanks for the years of work.

Example: When my father left the company after 40 years service, he received **a golden handshake**.

Put your money where your mouth is

Meaning: To do something rather than to just talk about it.

Example: Instead of talking about how sorry you feel for the poor, you should **put your money where your mouth is** and go out and do something to help them.

To live beyond your means

Meaning: If a person lives beyond their means, they spend more than what they can afford to spend or more than what they earn.

Example: He**'s living beyond his means**. He's bought a house that is far too expensive for him. If he isn't careful, the bank will repossess it.

Money for old rope

Meaning: This means earning money for doing a very simple task

Example: I bought some books at a charity sale for two pounds and resold them on the internet for two hundred pounds. It was **money for old rope**.

To be paid peanuts

Meaning: To earn a very low salary.

Example: I'm going to have to look for another job. I can't make ends meet. I**'m paid peanuts** in this one.

Money Idioms - Wealth

To be a fat cat

Meaning: Don't start visualizing a big fat cat. This expression has got nothing to do with a real cat. It refers to someone who has a lot of money

Example: He**'s a real fat cat**. He owns a lot of property.

To be in the money

Meaning: To have a lot of money, usually it refers to 'new money' just acquired

Example: He**'s really in the money**. Lately his standard of living has *gone right up. He's bought himself another flash car.

To be born with a silver spoon in your mouth

Meaning: When you are born into a rich family and want for nothing/have everything you desire and live an easy comfortable life.

Example: He's so lucky. His parents buy him everything he wants and he's got private tutors going to his house every afternoon. He won't even have to look for a job when he *grows up. He'll inherit his father's company. He really **was born with a silver spoon in his mouth**.

To be loaded

Meaning: To be full of money

Example: Her new boyfriend must **be really loaded**. He takes her to expensive restaurants every night.

To be rolling in it

Meaning: To have lots and lots of money (similar to 'be loaded')

Example: I don't know where Johnny gets all his money from. He**'s rolling in it**. He *eats out every night and *goes on a cruise once a month.

Money is no object

Meaning: To have no money problems whatsoever; you can buy what you want, when you want. (This has a similar meaning to the previous two idioms)

Example: **Money is no object** to her. She's always out buying new clothes every day.

Money to burn

Meaning: People who have 'money to burn' have so much money that they can buy whatever they want -the same as the above idiom 'money is no object'

Examples: A Ferrari is no problem for Johnny. He's got **money to burn**.

My son seems to think I've got **money to burn**. He's always asking me to buy him this, that and the next thing.

To have more money than sense

Meaning: When someone spends a lot of money on foolish things

Example: He spends a fortune on scratch cards. If you ask me, he**'s got more money than sense**. The expression 'if you ask me' in this context = if you want my opinion.

BE CAREFUL WITH YOUR MONEY IDIOMS

"A penny saved is a penny earned"

Every penny you do not spend is the same as having earned an extra penny

Look after the pennies and the pounds will take care of themselves

Meaning: This means that if you are careful not to make useless expenditures, the money saved by not spending, will soon *mount up.

Example: I've *given up my daily cup of coffee in the cafeteria. By the end of the year I will have saved about £500.

Penny wise - pound foolish

Meaning: This refers to someone who is very careful about spending when it comes to the small things. They may go to the cheapest supermarket to save a couple of pennies but *end up spending a fortune for something big.

Example: He walks for miles to buy all the special offers on at the various supermarkets, but when he saw that expensive car he couldn't resist buying it. He's **penny wise - pound foolish**.

VERY LITTLE MONEY IDIOMS

"Money never starts an idea. It is always the idea that starts the money".

To be living on the breadline

Meaning: When you only earn enough money to pay for your living expenses and you've got nothing left over.

Example: I'm *fed up with **living on the breadline**. I've never got any money to go out or to buy myself anything.

To make ends meet

Meaning: The same as 'to be living on the breadline'.

Example: My rent has *gone up and I'm finding it really difficult to **make ends meet**.

To be living on a shoestring

Meaning: The same as 'to be living on the breadline' and 'make ends meet'.

Example: I've **been living on a shoestring** for too long. It's time I found a job with a higher salary.

To live from hand to mouth

Meaning: The same as 'to be living on the breadline', 'make ends meet' and 'to be living on a shoestring.

No Money Idioms

"The best part about growing up with no money is that you know how to have fun without it".

To be broke

Meaning: To have no money

Example: "Can you lend me some money 'til Friday? 'I**'m broke**." "Sorry, I can't. I**'m broke** as well."

The idioms that follow have the same meaning.

To be hard up

Meaning: To have very little money

Example: I**'m really hard up** this month so I won't be able to spend any money.

To be strapped for cash

Meaning: The same as 'to be hard up'.

To not have two pennies to rub together

Meaning: This refers to a person who is very poor indeed.

Example: I can't go on holiday this year. I **haven't got two pennies to rub together**.

IDIOMS TO SAY THAT A PERSON IS MEAN

"A rich man who is stingy is the worst pauper"

~ Yiddish Proverb

Cheapskate

<u>Meaning</u>: Someone who never spends any money; usually they let other people pay for them.

The following expressions have exactly the same meaning as the one above.

To be stingy

<u>Meaning</u>: To never put your hand in your pocket

<u>Example</u>: He**'s so stingy**. He never puts his hand in his pocket.

His wife left him because of his stinginess.

To be tight-fisted

<u>Meaning</u>: The same as 'stingy'

Scrounger - A person who never spends but expects everyone else to pay for him/her. Usually they ask everyone else to pay for them or they continuously ask for cigarettes or they borrow things with no intention of *giving them <u>back</u>.

To scrounge off someone

<u>Meaning</u>: To make people or allow people to pay for you all the time. Normally someone who scrounges off another person pretends they do not have any money or pretends they have forgotten to bring money with them so as to make other people pay for them.

<u>Example</u>: He's always **scrounging off his friends** instead of paying for things himself. When we go to the pub, I am always the one who pays for him. Strangely enough he always seems to have mistakenly left his wallet at home. He's nothing but a scrounger.

TIME IDIOMS

"Man thinks he is killing time, it's really time that's killing man'

To kill time

Meaning: Do something just to pass the time.

Example: I arrived half an hour early for my dental appointment so I just walked around looking in shop windows **to kill time**.

To have the time of your life

Meaning: To really enjoy yourself.

Example: We **had the time of our lives** when we were on holiday.

To waste time

Meaning: Do something with no purpose.

Example: My son **wastes** so much **time** in front of the computer.

Just in the nick of time

Meaning: To get to a place or finish something just before it is too late.

Example: I thought I was going to miss my flight but the taxi driver got me to the airport **just in the nick of time**.

To hit the big time

Meaning: To become successful and maybe famous.

Example: He **hit the big time**, and *moved out of the neighbourhood. He felt too important to associate with his old friends.

Time's up

Meaning: This means there is no time left to do something. The time limit or deadline has been reached.

Example: **Time's up**. *Hand in your test papers.

A matter of time

Meaning: This is said before saying what you think will happen in the future.

Example: It's only **a matter of time** before that shop *closes down. They only have a couple of customers a day. Not enough to keep the place going.

Time after time

Meaning: Over and over again, repeatedly.

Example: Mother to son: "I've told you **time after time** to lock the door when you go out."

Time and time again

Meaning: This means exactly the same as 'time after time'.

Long time no see

Meaning: You say this when you meet someone you haven't seen for a long time.

Example: "Hi, **long time no see**. What have you *been up to?"

From time to time

Meaning: Occasionally.

Example: I meet my old school friends **from time to time**.

At all times

Meaning: Always.

Example: Airport announcements: "Passengers are reminded to keep their luggage with them **at all times**."

WEATHER IDIOMS

When it is raining very heavily, we use the following idiomatic expressions:

It's raining cats and dogs

It's pouring down

It's pouring from the heavens

It's bucketing down

It's flooding down

It's pissing down or it's peeing down very colloquial

To feel under the weather

Meaning: To not feel very well, or be tired or stressed.

Example: I'm not going to work today as I**'m feeling a bit under the weather**.

It never rains but it pours

Meaning: We use this idiom to say that one bad thing happens after another.

Example: First I got a huge electricity bill, then I broke my leg, then my wife left me and now I'm being evicted. **It never rains but it pours**.

Come rain or shine

Meaning: This means that nothing will stop you from doing something or going somewhere.

Example: Don't worry. I am definitely coming on Saturday. I'll be there **come rain or shine** (no matter what).

To save for a rainy day

Meaning: Put money aside in case of an emergency.

Example: I'm **saving for a rainy day**. You never know what's *round the corner. This is another idiom.*'You never know what's round the corner' means that 'anything unexpected can happen'.

To be snowed under

Meaning: To have too much work.

Example: I can't leave the office until late this evening because I**'m snowed under**.

To break the ice

Meaning: Say something to make people feel less nervous or embarrassed, and more relaxed especially in a social setting.

Example: He made a joke about the weather and everyone started laughing. That really **broke the ice**.

A ray of hope

Meaning: A small chance of something happening depending on luck - this expression is used in a positive sense.

Example: My lawyer told me there is **a ray of hope** that I will win the case. He thinks there is a little bit of a possibility

A ray of sunshine

Meaning: Something or someone who brings happiness into your life.

Example: My new puppy is **a ray of sunshine**. He has really *brightened up my life.

To make hay while the sun shines

Meaning: This means that you shouldn't *turn down a good opportunity, usually to earn money, as you never know; maybe tomorrow you won't be so lucky. Take advantage of a good opportunity when it arises.

Example: My boss has asked me to work on Sundays so I've accepted. I need to **make hay while the sun shines**.

The tip of the iceberg

Meaning: We use this expression to refer to a situation in which you or someone else can only see a small part of a more complex problem.

Example: The money laundering scandal is just **the tip of the iceberg**. Behind it there is seemingly a multimillion dollar drug ring.

To have your head in the clouds

Meaning: To walk around in a dream like state unaware of what is going on around you.

Example: The student wasn't paying attention to the lesson. His mind was elsewhere/he was thinking about other things. The teacher told him he would have to stop **having his head in the clouds** all the time if he wanted to pass his exams.

Every cloud has a silver lining

Meaning: Out of every bad situation comes some good. This idiom is used to comfort people who are *going through a difficult moment in their lives.

Example: Don't worry too much about losing your job. Maybe it was your destiny. There will be a much better job out there for you. Remember that **every cloud has a silver lining**.

Another idiom with the same meaning is:

After the rain comes the sunshine

Example: Relax and be happy that things are not going too well for you. This means that something good is going to happen. **After the rain comes the sunshine**.

There's a cloud on the horizon

Meaning: If you foresee a problem or difficulty that could happen in the future, then you use this expression.

Example: I can see **a cloud on the horizon**. Our biggest client is about to go bust and they still haven't paid for this year's huge order. If they *go bust then we risk *going under *along with them.

There's something in the wind

Meaning: When you sense something is going to happen.

Example: The boss is really nervous today. No doubt **there is something in the wind**.

To get a windfall

Meaning: To receive an unexpected source of money; usually quite substantial.

Example: I received an unexpected cheque from the income tax office; that was **a real windfall**.

A storm in a teacup

Meaning: To greatly over react to something that is not of great importance. You become angry for nothing.

Example: I caused **a real storm in a teacup** when I forgot to phone my girlfriend Jenny. She went absolutely crazy. I don't know what *came over her. She was screaming blue murder for hours after I met her. She didn't believe that I had forgotten. She suspected I was with another girl.

To have a face like thunder

Meaning: We use this expression when someone has a really angry expression on his or her face.

Example: Her **face was like thunder** when I told her I had broken her crystal vase.

To storm out

Meaning: Leave a place very angrily.

Example: She **stormed out** of the house and slammed the door behind her because her mother had accused her of something she hadn't done.

To weather the storm

Meaning: To experience and survive a difficult situation.

Example: I don't know how she manages to keep a smile on her face after all she's *been through. She really knows how to **weather the storm**.

To spring clean

Meaning: To give the house a good thorough (deep) cleaning; usually people do this in spring time, although it is used for any time of the year.

Example: I'm going to give the house a good **spring cleaning**. I haven't cleaned it properly for a long time.

To have an Indian summer

Meaning: When the weather is unexpectedly hot. This expression is used mainly for countries where the climate is not so good.

Example: Britain **had an Indian summer** last year. It was 35 degrees nearly every day.

A fair weather friend

Meaning: When someone is your friend only when everything is going well but stops being your friend the minute things start to go wrong in your life we use the expression.

Example: It's goodbye to you my **fair weather friend**. I never want to see you again. The minute I had a problem you stopped phoning me. It is better to lose a friend like you than keep you.

To stand about as much chance as a snowball in hell

Meaning: When you see the situation as impossible.

Example: I think I **stand about as much chance as a snowball in hell** of getting that job. I've got no qualifications.

WHAT YOU ARE TALKING ABOUT IDIOMS

When we don't understand what someone is saying, we can use any of the following expressions:

You're talking double Dutch.

You might as well be talking Chinese.

I haven't the foggiest idea what you are talking about.

I haven't got the faintest idea what you mean.

I've no idea what you're on about.

You're talking a load of mumbo jumbo.

You're talking bollocks.

I can't make head or tail of what you're on about.

What the heck are you on about?

What the blazes do you mean?

The following idioms are used when asking someone if he or she understands you.

Do you get the idea?

Do you get the message?

Do you get the picture?

Do you see what I mean?

Put someone in the picture

Meaning: To explain to someone what is happening/inform them of what is going on.

Example: The workers had no idea what was going to happen when the company was bought over. The manager called a meeting to **put them in the picture**.

FIXED EXPRESSIONS

Above and beyond

<u>Meaning</u>: More than what is necessary or expected/exceeding.

<u>Example</u>: Teachers who go **above and beyond** their normal duties by helping students out of hours make a huge impact on their lives. They connect with boys and girls and don't just stick to the curriculum.

All but

<u>Meaning</u>: Everyone or everything except.

<u>Example</u>: **All but** one boy arrived on time for the school outing.

All for

To be all for (something)

<u>Meaning</u>: You really want this to happen/you completely agree with it or you completely agree to with someone else to do something.

<u>Example</u>: I know he doesn't have the qualifications but he does have the experience. He's worked in the sector before. I **am all for** giving him a chance.

"We're *<u>going out</u> now to have a pizza. Would you like to come with us?" "Oh yes, I**'m all for** it."

All the better

Meaning: This phrase is used when something is better than expected.

Example: "Did you know our new secretary can speak Spanish as well as German?"

"No I didn't. I thought she could only speak German. **All the better**. Now she can communicate with our clients in Spain."

All of a sudden

Meaning: Without any warning.

Example: **All of a sudden** it started to rain. It was completely unexpected as the sun had been shining all day. Needless to say none of us had brought an umbrella with us.

All out to

Meaning: To make every possible effort to do something.

Example: He**'s all out to** prove he's a great football player. Look at him with that ball, he is just fantastic.

As a last resort

Meaning: Do something only when all other attempts have been tried without results.

Example: Couples who are trying to have children, say they view adoption **as a last resort**.

As a matter of fact

Meaning: Believe it or not.

Example: A: "Giovanni can't speak English so it is no good sending him abroad on the assignment."

B: "**As a matter of fact** he can. He's been having English lessons for the past few months and he can speak reasonably well now. He'll manage quite well abroad."

As a matter of principle

Meaning: To have a moral belief for not doing something.

Example: **As a matter of principle** I'm not buying any clothes from that store again. I know they sell them at a good price and they are fashionable, but they use sweatshops in third world countries. These poor people work night and day for paltry earnings.

As a rule

Meaning: This is generally true most of the time.

Example: **As a rule** I never drink coffee in the evenings. The caffeine in it keeps me awake.

As far as I'm concerned

Meaning: This expression is used when the speaker states his/her own point of view.

Example: **As far as** I'm concerned, Italian food is the best in the world.

As for

Meaning: With regards to/regarding.

Note: We use "as for" + pronoun/noun.

Example: It's getting late. I'm going to *head off home now. **As for** you Mary, you can stay a bit longer seeing you don't have to *get up early tomorrow like I do.

As well as

Meaning: Not only ... but also/not only A but also B.

Examples: When you join the club, (become a member) you can choose to play football **as well as** rugby.

There will be winners **as well as** losers if Greece leaves the euro.

There is a proverb in English which says: Some people cannot see the trees for the forest. It is important to see the trees **as well as** the forest.

Note: When "**as well as**" is followed by a verb, the verb takes the gerund form. This is because "as" is a preposition and in English, verbs which come immediately after a preposition, always take the gerund.

<u>Example</u>: **As well as** listening to music in my free time, I also read books.

Another way of saying the above sentences without changing the meaning is:

Not only can you choose to play football, but you can also choose to play rugby.

Not only will there be winners if Greece leaves the euro, but there will also be losers.

Not only is it important to see the forest, but it is also important to see the trees.

Not only do I listen to music in my free time, but I also read books.

<u>Important note</u>:

We must not confuse the idiomatic meaning of "**as well as**" with its non idiomatic use.

Non idiomatic use of "**as well as**"

There are some jobs which robots will never be able to do **as well as** humans.

<u>Meaning</u>: Humans will do a better job.

I do my job **as well as** I possibly can.

<u>Meaning</u>: I do my job in the best possible way.

These "non idiomatic" uses, as seen previously are used in what some languages call the "inverted comparison". When A + B are equal or when used with "not" then "A is less than B"

"Well" is the adverb which stems from the adjective "good".

I do a good job.

I do my job well.

I do my job **as well as** I can.

My father is well. (In good health)

He (A) is **as well as** my mother (B) = both are well. We compare his state of "wellness" to that of another, in this case, "my mother" - A+B are equal.

He is not **as well as** my mother. = my mother is better (in better health than he is) A is less than B

Look at the following examples. Out of context they are ambiguous. They have double meaning but in the context we understand if the speaker is using the idiomatic meaning of "**as well as**" or if he/she is using the "non idiomatic meaning".

1) I speak English **as well as** Italian. (Idiomatic meaning) - not only do I speak English but I also speak Italian. I speak both languages.

2) I speak English **as well as** Italian. (Non idiomatic meaning) - I speak both languages equally well. I do not speak English better than I speak Italian and I do not speak Italian better than I speak English.

We could take away the ambiguity of the first example by rearranging (changing) the word order.

Example: **As well as** English I speak Italian. This clarifies the meaning more.

As long As

Meaning: On the condition that.

Example: You can use my car **as long as** you're careful with it = you can use my car on the condition that you are careful with it.

You can go to the disco tonight with your friends **as long as** you're back home by midnight.

"**As long as**" similarly to "**as well as**" has its 'non idiomatic' meaning.

Example: My table is **as long as** yours = both our tables are the same length. Table A and table B are the same length.

As yet

Meaning: Until now/so far/up to this present moment.

Example: **As yet**, I have been unable to contact him. His phone is always engaged.

At all

Meaning: This expression adds emphasis in questions and negatives. It gives them a stronger meaning.

Not even in the least/in no way whatsoever

Example: You think I am selfish but really I am not like that **at all**.

*See also **not at all**

At the end of the day

Meaning: After all is said and done/in the end.

Example: We can complain all we want about how little we are paid, but **at the end of the day** we are lucky to have a job in this day and age.

Before you know it

Meaning: When something happens so quickly you do not even realise it.

Examples: The years pass by so quickly that **before you know it** you look in the mirror and old age is staring you right in the face.

That new express train is super fast. We *got on it in London and **before we knew it** we were in Edinburgh.

One minute it's summer then **before you know it**, it's Christmas. Doesn't time fly so quickly?

Before long

Meaning: Very soon.

Example: On the phone: "I'm nearly at the station now. I'll see you **before long**."

Better Off

Used with 'be'

Meaning: To be in a more comfortable, convenient and more pleasant position.

Examples: I'd **be better off** without him. He doesn't love me. He treats me so badly.

I'm better off now than what I was last year. I earn more money and I live in a nicer flat.

I'd **be better off** going to work by train than by car. I always get stuck in traffic jams.

Between one thing and another

Meaning: One thing has happened and so have others. This means that with all the things that are happening to you, you are stressed or distracted or going crazy.

Example: I've got so many things to do these days. **Between one thing and another** I feel I am going to go crazy.

Beyond belief

<u>Meaning</u>: Unbelievable.

<u>Example</u>: It's **beyond belief** how much he spends every month.

By all accounts

<u>Meaning</u>: When we use this expression we believe something to be true by what we have heard from others.

<u>Example</u>: She is, **by all accounts**, an excellent hairdresser.

By the way

<u>Meaning</u>: This expression is used to introduce something into the conversation; something that the speaker or the listener just remembered.

<u>Example</u>: Oh **by the way**! I forgot to mention. I won't be able to make it to the dinner on Saturday evening.

Come to that

<u>Meaning</u>: This means, "while we are on the subject", something which has just *<u>come into</u> mind is triggered by something said in the conversation.

<u>Example</u>: A is speaking to B: "I'm going to have to *<u>call in</u> a gardener. The garden is a complete mess.

"**Come to that**, you said you'd help me clean it up. Don't you remember?"

Few and far between

Meaning: To happen on rare occasions at large intervals of time.

Example: The times that my daughter has cleaned her room are **few and far between**. I can count them on one hand.

For heaven's sake

Meaning: This expression denotes annoyance and/or frustration.

Example: "**For heaven's sake** go and do your homework. I'm not telling you again." said the father to his disobedient son. "When will you learn to *do as you are told."

*Do as you are told = obey

Go out of one's way

Meaning: Do everything possible.

Examples: He **goes out of his way** to help people. He's such a considerate person.

He **went out of his way** to ruin my holiday by arguing over trivial matters.

Grin and bear it

Meaning: Accept something bad without complaining about it/be patient until it is over.

Example: It's been tough trying to pay this huge fine I got but I will just have to **grin and bear it**.

If I may say so

Meaning: This expression means 'I hope you don't mind if I say this/I hope it is not a problem for me to say this/I hope I have your permission to say what I said'. It is a very polite expression to use.

Example: You look beautiful today **if I may say so**.

In due course

Meaning: This expression means that something will happen at the appropriate time (when the time is right) and you need to be patient as no one can make it happen sooner.

Example: In reply to a letter submitted for a job:

We will inform you **in due course** if your application has been successful.

It just goes to show

Meaning: This expression more or less means: it just proves that/it just makes you realise.

Example: There was a sudden downpour of rain yesterday and I didn't have my umbrella with me. **It just goes to show** you should never *go out without your umbrella. British weather is very unpredictable.

Her husband left her after thirty years without warning. She never ever suspected anything was wrong with their relationship. **It just goes to show** you can never be 100 % sure of anyone.

Every time I don't check my change at the supermarket, I get *short changed. When I do check it, I am never short changed. **It just goes to show** that you should always check your change.

*To short change (someone) = to give a customer less change than what you should. I give the cashier £20. I spend £16 and she gives me my change. There is only £3 instead of £4, so she has short changed me by £1.

It's about time

Meaning: The moment has arrived that you really need to do something without further delay

We use **it's about time + past tense** of verb, even if we are speaking in the present or referring to the future.

Example: **It's about time** you <u>saw</u> a dentist. Your teeth are beginning to decay. You're going to *<u>end up</u> losing them if you're not careful.

It's about time I <u>got</u> a new washing machine. This one doesn't spin anymore. The clothes come out dripping wet.

It's about time we <u>started</u> to move. It's getting late and if we don't go now we could miss the train.

Not at all

<u>Meaning</u>: You are welcome, don't mention it. Used in response to someone who thanks you for something. It is also used to mean "not in the least bit/not very"

<u>Example</u>: Person A: "Thanks for helping me with the cleaning." Person B: "**Not at all**!"

I'm **not at all** happy about my brother coming to visit me. We argue nonstop. If I say something is black, then he'll say it is white. We just don't *<u>get on</u> and we never will. It's a fact of life.

Not all that

<u>Meaning</u>: Not very (Used in the negative)

<u>Example</u>: She's **not all that** intelligent. This means the same as "She isn't very intelligent."

Make my day

Meaning: This expression is used when someone says or does something that makes you feel a sudden sense of happiness.

Examples: He really **made my day** when he told me that he wanted to marry me.

He really **made my day** when he told me I looked much younger than what I really am.

Make up your mind

Meaning: Decide.

Example: **Make up your mind** what you want to do. It's getting late.

I couldn't **make up my mind** what dress to wear to the party. In the end I chose my pink flowery one.

Might as well/may as well

Meaning: [1]This indicates a reluctance/unwillingness to do something but in that moment there is nothing better to do.

[2]It would be better to do this.

[3]Hypothetically (in the past) indicating that it would have been better to do something else rather than do what you did.

Examples: [1]I **might as well** go to bed. There is nothing on the TV.

[2]You **might as well** tell me what happened because sooner or later I will find out .

[3]I **might as well have stayed** at home last night as the party was crap. (It would have been better for me to have stayed at home)

I might have known

Meaning: Used to indicate that the speaker is not in the least bit surprised about something

Example: **I might have known** he would have told everyone. (It comes as no surprise to me that he told everyone/he told everyone and this does not surprise me) this is a present statement about something in the past.

Never mind

Meaning: [1]It's not important/it doesn't matter/there is no need to worry. [2]To never be bothered or concerned.

Examples: [1]"Sorry, what did you say?" **Never mind**, it was nothing important." (Forget I said it)

[2]I **never mind** where we go on holiday. As long as I get a break from my somewhat boring routine, I am happy.

On my account

<u>Meaning</u>: For me/for my sake

<u>Example</u>: Please do it **on my account**. I know you don't want to, but you would be doing me a huge favour.

On no account

<u>Meaning</u>: This expression indicates strict prohibition/absolutely not allowed/you must not do this

<u>Example</u>: "**On no account** must you cross that busy road," said the mother to her young son. "You could get killed. The cars go very fast."

In English we can add the word "whatsoever" after the expression "on no account" to give added emphasis.

<u>Example</u>: "**On no account whatsoever** should you play with matches," said the mother to her young son. "You could burn yourself or even worse, burn the house down."

Of one's own accord

<u>Meaning</u>: To do something because you want to do it, not because anyone asked you to do it or forced you to do it.

<u>Example</u>: Nobody forced Alex to leave his job. He did it **of his own accord**. Now he is paying the

consequences for his own actions. He's having difficulty in finding another job.

On the other hand

Meaning: This signals an alternative viewpoint.

Example: Living in the city has its advantages such as cinemas, nightlife and better job prospects but **on the other hand** it can be stressful. There is a lot of noise, traffic, pollution to name but a few. That is why I am now thinking about moving to the country.

Once and for all

Meaning: Finally in a permanent way.

Example: The Greek state has decided to *crackdown on tax evasion **once and for all** which is costing the nation thousands of Euros in uncollected taxes.

Over and above

Meaning: In addition/besides.

Example: **Over and above** having to work, I have a family to *look after and a home to run.

It's pointless

Meaning: To be a waste of time/make no sense

Example: **It's pointless** trying to keep the house clean when my children dirty it all the time.

It's pointless arguing with him. You are onto a losing battle. He's a very unreasonable person.

Put an end to

Meaning: Stop.

Example: I've **put an end to** my husband coming home late every evening. I've told him to go. He can go back to his mother's.

Settle for less

Meaning: Accept something that is not really what you wish for.

Example: I went to see a house today. It isn't as nice as the one I live in now so I have decided not to take it. Why should I **settle for less**?

So to speak

Meaning: This is a figurative expression which emphasizes the fact that you do not mean something in the literal sense. Often it is used with irony and sarcasm.

Example: There's a mouse in the house, **so to speak**. All the chocolate biscuits seem to disappear. (This is figurative because really there is no mouse. Here we mean that someone in the house is acting (behaving) in the same way as a mouse by sneaking food. "Sneak" means to do something in a hidden way.

Guest to host: "This food is delicious. Who cooked it?"

Host to Guest: (Pointing to her husband) "the chef **so to speak**." (Her husband is not really a chef)

A similar expression is: "**as it were**".

Stand a chance

Meaning: If someone stands a chance, it means they have a possibility. If a person doesn't stand a chance, then it means the opposite. He/she has no possibility.

Examples: You don't **stand a chance** of winning the beauty contest. You've *put on too much weight.

A: "Do you think I **stand a chance** of getting the job I'm going for today?"

B:"Yes, I really think you do. You've got the right qualifications."

Take advantage of

Meaning: Take the opportunity to use something or someone for your own personal profit/ gain/also for negative selfish motives.

Example: I **took advantage of** the fact that the supermarket was selling three chickens for the price of two. I bought nine therefore three were free.

She **takes advantage of** her boyfriend's kind heart. She lets him pay for everything. (Selfish motives)

There is no such thing as/there is such a thing as

Meaning: It does not exist/it exists.

Example: Some say **there is no such thing as** darkness. There is such a thing as absence of light.

To some extent

Meaning: Up to a certain degree/point. (Partially)

Example: I agree with you **to some extent**.

To tell you the truth

Meaning: Give your honest opinion.

Example: **To tell you the truth** I would rather not *go out tonight.

To be honest with you

"To be honest with you" has the same meaning as "to tell you the truth"

Meaning: To say what you honestly think.

Example: **To be honest with you**, I don't really like Jean's husband.

SIMILES

What is a simile?

A simile uses figurative language to compare two things which are different. We use 'as' or 'like' with similes. The word 'simile' means 'similar to'.

Example:

He can swim like a fish

He can swim so well that we compare him to a fish.

Many similes have deeply rooted origins and many others are used based on the sound. Alliteration is common in similes.

What is alliteration?

Alliteration is a grammatical term meaning two or more words in a row starting with the same sounds.

Example:

In the "Wizard of Oz", we had the "Wicked Witch of the West".

Similes with "like and as"

To be like a bear with a sore head

Meaning: When you are tired and irritable and nobody can say anything to you without you getting upset and *snapping at them

Example: The boss is **like a bear with a sore head** today. It is better not to approach him. Wait until tomorrow when he's in a better mood.

Like death warmed up

Meaning: When someone looks terrible, maybe because he or she is ill or maybe they haven't slept well, then we describe them by using this simile.

Example: Person A: "John looks **like death warmed up** today."

Person B: "Yes I know. He's got a terrible hangover. He was at a party last night and *overdid it with the drink."

*Exaggerated with the alcohol

To cut like a knife

Meaning: When something 'cuts like a knife', it causes you great emotional pain.

Example: It really **cuts like a knife** to know that my boyfriend doesn't love me anymore.

To croak like a frog

Meaning: When you have a really sore throat and it affects your voice, we compare the croaking noise to that of a frog.

Example: "How is Jill?"

"She is not very well at all. She was **croaking like a frog** on the phone this morning. I couldn't understand a word of what she was saying."

Drink like a fish

Meaning: This refers to someone who is on their way to becoming an alcoholic.

Example: Person A: "I saw John in the pub last night. He was staggering all over the place. He had had a lot to drink." Person B: "Yes I know. He's been **drinking like a fish** since he lost his job."

To eat like a bird

Meaning: This refers to someone who doesn't eat much. Just like a bird that pecks at its food.

Example: Person A: "John looks so thin these days."

Person B: "Yes I know. He's been **eating like a bird** since the day he lost his job."

To eat like a horse

Meaning: This has the opposite meaning to 'eat like a bird'. When someone has a large appetite we often use this simile.

Example: Person A: "Margaret's *put on a lot of weight since the last time I saw her."

Person B: "She's been **eating like a horse**, that's why."

To eat like a pig

Meaning: This simile is used to describe a person who is always eating everything he/she sees. There is no stopping them.

Example: My daughter is getting fatter and fatter. She **eats like a pig**. Last night she devoured about four bars of chocolate and three packets of crisps whilst watching the TV, and that was after she had had her dinner.

To fit like a glove

Meaning: When something fits you so well (a perfect fit) that it seems to have been tailored made especially for you.

Example: In the shoe shop:

Shop assistant: "Are the shoes the right size madam?"

Customer: "Yes, I'll take them. They **fit like gloves**."

To have eyes like a hawk

Meaning: This means that you quickly notice what is *going on around you.

A hawk is a bird with exceptionally good eyesight. When we use this simile, we compare a person's eyesight to that of a hawk.

Examples: You need **eyes like a hawk** when *looking after my two year old grandson. He's always up to something. Yesterday he nearly threw my keys down the drain while I was talking to my neighbour. Luckily I noticed just in time.

You need to have **eyes like a hawk** to be a good body guard.

We can also use '**to watch someone like a hawk**'. This means you watch them very closely without taking your eyes off someone or something for a moment.

Example: Person A: "Can you take my puppy to the park this afternoon. I am working. Please make sure he doesn't *run away."

Person B: "Don't worry; I'll **watch him like a hawk**."

My boss **watches us all like a hawk**. We can't even go to the toilet without him noticing.

To have a memory like a sieve

Meaning: This means that you keep forgetting everything. A sieve is full of tiny holes so a person's memory is thought of as having many tiny holes which lets everything slip out.

Example: A: "Where did you park the car?"

B: "Oh gosh! I don't remember."

A: "You**'ve got a memory like a sieve** these days. You can't seem to remember anything."

To hit you like a ton of bricks

Meaning: If something not so good happens very unexpectedly then it '**hits you like a ton of bricks**', like sudden shocking news.

Example: When she *found out that her 'so called sister' was actually her mother, it **hit her like a ton of bricks**.

To leap like a frog

Meaning: To jump up very high.

Example: He **leapt up into the air like a frog** when his lottery numbers *came up. "We've won the lottery, he cried out to his wife."

To run like the wind

Meaning: This refers to a person who is a very fast runner.

Example: That American athlete can really **run like the wind**. He is amazing.

To shake like a leaf

Meaning: This is used to describe a reaction when intense fear is felt.

Example: I was really **shaking like a leaf** when the boss called me into his office. I thought he was going to sack me for my late time-keeping but it *turned out he wanted to put me in line for promotion. What a relief! All that panic and anxiety was for nothing.

To sleep like a log

Meaning: This means that you sleep very well.

Example: A: "Did you hear the storm during the night?"

B: "No I didn't. I **slept like a log** all night."

To sting like a bee

Meaning: A bee sting hurts you physically. This simile is also used to describe emotional pain.

Examples: It really **stung like a bee** to *find out my husband had betrayed me.

Her words really **stung like a bee**. I will never forget what she said to me.

To work like clockwork

Meaning: If something works like clockwork, then it works perfectly well with no irregularities.

Example: My old radio is now about fifty years old but it still **works like clockwork**.

As agile as a monkey

Monkeys are agile animals that are able to swing from tree to tree with so much ease.

Example: That new Swedish gymnast is **as agile as a monkey**.

As alike as two peas in a pod/like two peas in a pod

Meaning: This means that two people look almost the same. They are so alike that at times you find it difficult to tell one from the other. Peas are identical so if you have two peas, it's impossible to tell which one is which.

Example: He and his brother are **as alike as two peas in a pod**. I never know which one is which. They even have the same voices.

It is also common to say: He and his brother are **like two peas in a pod**.

To be as black as coal

Meaning: Completely black or very dirty.

Example: His eyes are **as black as coal**.

Mother to son: "Go and get washed. You are **as black as coal**. Have you been playing in the mud again?"

As blind as a bat

Meaning: When your eyesight is not as good as it once was.

Example: She's **as blind as a bat**. She thought that old black bag on the chair was the cat. She'll need to get stronger glasses.

As bold as brass

Meaning: A shameless and overconfident person who acts without caring about the consequences of his/her actions. This kind of person does not feel embarrassment in situations where others would feel mortified.

Example: You need to be **as bold as brass** to go up to people in the street and ask them for money.

Origin:

The first known user is believed to be Shakespeare. Some people believe that the simile "**as bold as brass**" was inspired nineteen years before Shakespeare, in 1770 by Brass Crosby, Chief London magistrate and mayor.

Brass is a shiny hard metal that was often referred to as cheap and vulgar being a poor imitation to gold.

As brave as a lion

Meaning: When we compare a person's bravery to that of a lion; lions are large animals that tend not to be afraid of anything.

Example: My little son is usually terrified of going to the dentist's, but today he was **as brave as a lion**.

As bright as a button

Meaning: This simile is a pun. A pun is a play on words, as the word "bright" can mean both shiny and clever.

When we say that a person is "**as bright as a button**", we mean they are intelligent and smart -they understand things very quickly.

The repetition of the 'b' makes this simile alliterative which means using the same letter or sound at the beginning of words that are close together.

As broad as it's long

Meaning: This means that it is difficult to decide which of two options to choose from as they are both the same. There is no difference between them. Similar to the saying, 'it's six of one and half a dozen of the other. Half a dozen = six.

Broad = the breadth of something and 'long' = the length. So when the length and the breadth are the same, they are equal.

Example:

Person A: "If we *take on that new project we can earn an extra £10,000 dollars, but there is one drawback. We will *fall into the higher tax bracket and *end up paying most of it on tax. What do you suggest we do?"

Person B: "There won't be much financial loss if we decide not to take it on. It is **as broad as it is long**." (The outcome is the same - or almost the same - whether we work on the project or not)

As brown as a berry

This is mainly used to describe someone with a very tanned skin.

Example: When he *came back from his holiday in Greece, he was **as brown as a berry**.

The origin of "**as brown as a berry**" goes back to Chaucer's "Canterbury Tales"

"His palfrey (saddle horse) was **as brown as a berry**".

Brown as a berry, short, and thickly made,

With black hair that he combed right prettily.

*Berries are not brown but in the days of Chaucer, it is thought that when he spoke about "berries", he was referring to whole, ungrounded grains, such as wheat berry, sometimes referred to as berries.

As busy as a bee

Meaning: When we use this simile, we compare ourselves to bees. Bees are busy creatures. They make about forty trips a day gathering nectar and pollen. They never stop and after about six weeks they have worked themselves to death.

Example: Every time I phone Jenny she never seems to have any time to talk. She is always **as busy as a bee**.

As changeable as the weather

Meaning: Often used to describe a person's mood.

Examples: John was so irritable today. I never know what mood he is going to be in. He's **as changeable as the weather**.

Mary can't make up her mind about which holiday to book. One day she wants to go to Spain, the next it's Italy and the next again she wants to stay in England. She's **as changeable as the weather**.

As clear as a bell

Meaning: When we hear a bell ring, the sound is very clear. Here we compare our understanding to the clear sound of a bell.

Example: A: "Did you understand everything that was said at the meeting." B: "Yes I did. The chairman was **as clear as a bell**."

As cold as ice

Meaning: This simile refers mainly to a person's character. It can refer to an unfriendly person or a cold and callous person.

Examples: A: "Did you meet the boss's wife at the staff dance?" B: "Yes I did but I didn't like her. She wasn't very friendly at all. In fact she was **as cold as ice**."

My last boyfriend was **as cold as ice** when he left me. No explanation, he just left.

As comfortable as an old pair of slippers

Meaning: This normally refers to a long standing relationship usually between husband and wife. You know each other so well both inside and out and are so familiar with each other's habits that you feel so comfortable in the relationship.

Example: They've been together for over fifty years. They are **as comfortable as an old pair of slippers** when they are together.

It can also refer to something comfortable- so comfortable that we compare it to old slippers

Example: I love this armchair. It's **as comfortable as an old pair of slippers**.

As common as muck

Meaning: This refers to a rough, vulgar, uneducated person with no cultural background.

Example: A: "Have you noticed how much Ruth *swears every time she opens her mouth?"B: "Yes I have. She's **as common as muck**."

This expression is not very polite as it implies that the person uttering it feels superior.

*To swear = to use foul language. It also means to solemnly promise, usually before the judge in a courtroom.

As cool as a cucumber

Meaning: This means to be very calm and composed in a difficult situation.

Example: Even when the prime minister lost the elections, he **was as cool as a cucumber**.

This simile probably originated from the fact that the inside of cucumbers is always cool to the touch.

As cunning as a fox

Meaning: When someone is as cunning as a fox, they can be very devious. They are able to *trick people into getting what they want.

Example: Don't trust John. He's **as cunning as a fox**.

As daft as a brush

Meaning: A silly foolish person

Example: John's behaviour makes him seem **as daft as a brush** when in reality he's quite the opposite.

As dark as a dungeon

Meaning: Dungeons are always very dark so this is where this simile derives from.

Example: "It's **as dark as a dungeon** in here. Can you *switch on the light please? I can't see where I am going."

As different as chalk and cheese

Meaning: When two people are opposites and have nothing in common we compare them to chalk and cheese.

Example: I don't know why they got married. They are **as different as chalk and cheese**. But then again, they do say that opposites attract.

Another variation: **As different as night and day**

As easy as ABC

Meaning: When we find something very easy to do we use this simile.

Example: A: "How did your exam go?" B: "Great! It was **as easy as ABC**."

We can also say 'as easy as 1 2 3'.

As fit as a fiddle

Meaning: This refers to a person's health, when he or she is fit and healthy.

Example: A: "How is your father now? The last time I spoke to him he had a bad dose of the flu. I hope he's feeling better now." B: "He's completely recovered. Now he's **as fit as a fiddle**."

As flat as a pancake

Meaning: To be very flat.

Example: I forgot to add baking powder to the cake mix. Now the cake is **as flat as a pancake**.

As free as a bird

Meaning: To feel completely free from any kind of ties.

Example: Now that I've left that boring job I feel **as free as a bird**. I don't have to listen to that boss giving me orders from morning until night.

As fresh as a daisy

Meaning: This is used to describe someone who is full of energy and enthusiasm especially after a good night's sleep.

Example: A: "I'm so tired after working all day."
B: "You should go to bed early tonight then. That way you'll be **as fresh as a daisy** tomorrow morning."

As good as gold

Meaning: This simile is used to describe a person's behaviour - when their behaviour is exceptionally good.

Example: Mother to babysitter: "How did little John behave today?"

Babysitter to mother: "He was **as good as gold**." (He behaved perfectly well)

As graceful as a swan

<u>Meaning</u>: To display grace and elegance; gracefulness belongs more to posture and motion rather than to beauty.

Swans seem to glide along the water with such grace.

<u>Example</u>: The figure skater glided along the ice **as graceful as a swan**.

As greedy as a pig

<u>Meaning</u>: When you have an excessive desire for things especially food.

<u>Example</u>: She's **as greedy as a pig**. She had four portions of ice cream today.

As happy as a lark

<u>Meaning</u>: To be extremely happy.

The bird song of the lark is melodious and cheerful which we attribute to happiness. When a person is very happy, we compare them to the happiness which the bird song eludes.

Example: Sally was **as happy as a lark** when her boyfriend sent her twelve red roses. It was completely unexpected of him.

If a person has a beautiful singing voice, we say: He/she sings like a lark.

As hard as nails

Meaning: This refers to a person who has no sympathy or mercy towards other people. This kind of person is hard hearted.

Example: My boss is **as hard as nails**. She reduced the new office junior to tears today after she had lost a document. Even when the girl apologized she still showed no pity towards her.

As heavy as lead

Meaning: This simile is used to describe very heavy things. Lead is known for its heaviness.

Example: Don't try to move that box. It's **as heavy as lead**. You could do yourself an injury. Wait until John gets back and he will help you.

When we are really tired it is quite common to say that your eyelids are as heavy as lead.

Example: If I don't go to bed I'm going to end up falling asleep in front of the TV. My eyelids are **as heavy as lead**.

As high as a kite

Meaning: When someone has taken drugs we refer to them as 'being high' so we compare them to a kite which flies high into the sky

Example: He was **as high as a kite** when I saw him. He must have been on drugs.

As hungry as a wolf

Meaning: A comparison is made between a person and a wolf. This simile indicates that the person is very hungry indeed. Wolves tend to eat a lot and very ferociously.

Example: Let's go and get something to eat. I'm **as hungry as a wolf**. The way I'm feeling right now I could eat anything.

As innocent or as gentle as a lamb

Meaning: Any person who is innocent or gentle as a lamb. It can also imply a naive or victimised person.

Lambs are young sheep and are seen as pure and innocent.

Example: It is impossible to believe that John committed the crime. He looks **as innocent as a lamb**. It's true what they say. 'You can't judge a book by its cover.'

As large as life

Meaning: When you are very surprised to see someone, then this is the simile to use, especially when reporting to another.

Example: At the pop concert today, Johnny Ratkins appeared on stage **as large as life**. It was a great surprise. We just couldn't believe our eyes. They did mention a mystery guest but never would we have thought it would be him.

As light as a feather

Meaning: When something or someone is very light we compare it or he/she to a feather.

Example: My new racing bike is pencil thin and **as light as a feather**. I can lift it with my pinkie. (Little finger)

As merry as the month of May

Meaning: The month of May is seen as a merry month because it is the start of springtime. The sun shines, flowers bloom and everyone is in a good mood. This is where this simile derives from.

Example: A: "The boss was in a really good mood today. I wonder what *came over him." B: "Yes I heard him whistling in the lift. He seemed **as merry as the month of May**."

As miserable as sin

Meaning: This refers to a person who is very unhappy. Someone who walks around with a miserable look on his/her face all the time. This type of person is never seen smiling or laughing and if anyone else is happy, this makes them even more miserable. They feel everyone should be unhappy like them.

Example: I don't like that new neighbour who's moved in next door to me. He's **as miserable as sin**.

As nice as nine pence

Meaning: When someone is very nice towards you, we use this simile to describe their attitude.

Example: A: "I'm not sure if I like that shop assistant in the bakery round the corner." B: "She is always **as nice as nine pence** to me."

As old as the hills

Meaning: Very old.

Example: "Mum, that's a nice coat you're wearing." "Really! Do you like it? It's **as old as the hills**. I've had it since I was a teenager."

As plain as day

Meaning: When something is very obvious.

Example: If the government raises taxes again, many more people will fall below the poverty line. Why can't they see this? It's **as plain as day**.

As playful as a kitten

Meaning: Full of high spirits and having the desire to play.

Example: My elderly dog is **as playful as a kitten**. You would never believe he is almost 16 years old.

As pleased as Punch

Meaning: A person who has a feeling of self satisfaction or delight.

Example: He was **as pleased as Punch** the day he was awarded a gold Olympic medal.

This expression was used by Charles Dickens in 'Hard Times', 1854; when Sissy got into the school here, her father was as pleased as Punch.

It originates to the puppets "Punch and Judy" which performed on the beaches of England to entertain children. Punch was a very proud and self satisfied puppet. The "Punch and Judy" show was of Italian origin but over the years has changed.

As poor as a church mouse

Meaning: Extremely poor.

Example: He is **as poor as a church mouse**. He cannot even afford to buy himself shoes. He's been walking around with holes in the soles of his shoes for months.

As pretty as a picture

Meaning: Very pretty.

Example: She looked **as pretty as a picture** today in that new flowery dress she was wearing.

As proud as a peacock

Meaning: This simile implies having a very high opinion of oneself. It refers to the male peacock with his colourful tail which when courting, (looking to mate a female) expands like a fan to reveal the most beautiful colours. This has long been symbolized as vanity and pride.

Origin:

Chaucer used this expression in 'The Reeve's Tail: "As any peacock, he was proud and gay (merry, happy, delighted -the original meaning of the adjective 'gay').

As quick as a flash

Meaning: If you do something as quick as a flash, you do it very quickly, in less than a second.

Example: I didn't even see the cat stealing the fish. It must have jumped up on the table and grabbed it **as quick as a flash**.

Other variations of 'as quick as a flash' are as follows:

As quick as silver

This simile is used because 'quicksilver -mercury' is so quick at moving that it is impossible to hold it.

We use this in a similar way to 'as quick as a flash'.

As quick as a wink

Meaning: It takes less than a second to wink so this is why we use this expression.

Similar to 'as quick as a flash' and 'as quick as a silver'

As red as a cherry

Meaning: Anything/anyone of a blood red colour can be compared to cherries.

Example: He was **as red as a cherry** after sitting in the sun all afternoon.

Other variations include:

As red as a berry

As red as a lobster

As regular as clockwork

Meaning: The mechanisms inside a clock tick away at a regular timing. When we say something is as regular as clockwork, we mean that it is reliable. Something we can *count on.

Example: Companies rely on their customers to be **as regular as clockwork** with their payments.

As right as rain

Meaning: This means that everything is going to be all right be it an illness or a situation.

Examples: I didn't feel too well but after a couple of days rest, I felt **as right as rain**.

Things weren't going too well when sales dropped in the last quarter, but now things are picking up so it looks as though everything is going to be as right as rain.

Origins of this simile:

This expression has been around since medieval times originating in Britain, where rainy weather is a normal fact of life. W.L. Philips once wrote, "The expression, "**as right as rain**" surely must have been invented by an Englishman.

Rain was considered to be 'right' probably because it is perceived as something good which causes growth. Without rain, crops cannot grow.

Its alliteration is pleasing to the ear. **R + R** (**R**ight as **R**ain)

As safe as the bank of England

<u>Meaning</u>: To be safe and secure.

Banks are (or were) considered safe places to leave your money or deposit your valuables; this expression probably derived from this fact.

<u>Example</u>:

Person A: "Can you *<u>look after</u> my jewellery while I am on holiday? I would be too worried to leave it in case burglars *<u>break in</u> while I'm away."

Person B: "Don't worry you can leave it with me. It will be **as safe as the bank of England**. I am always at home so there is no chance of anyone *<u>breaking into</u> my place."

As sharp as a razor

<u>Meaning</u>: This simile refers to a quick thinking intelligent person.

<u>Example</u>: My grandfather is almost 98 years old but he is still **as sharp as razor**.

As sick as a dog

<u>Meaning</u>: This means to be very ill indeed

<u>Example</u>: I couldn't go to work this morning because I was **as sick as a dog** all night.

Other variations are: As sick as a parrot

As silent as a grave

<u>Meaning</u>: This is usually used to make a promise not to tell anyone a secret that has been told to you.

<u>Example</u>: A: "Please don't tell anyone what I told you. I don't want anyone to *<u>find out</u> what I did."

B: "Don't worry. I will be **as silent as a grave**. You *have my word for it."

*You have my word for it = I promise

As small as an ant

Meaning: Ants are tiny little creatures so when something is extremely small (tiny) we compare it to an ant.

Example: When my sister's baby was born she was **as small as an ant**. She had to stay in an incubator for several weeks.

As slippery as an eel

Meaning: This simile is used to refer to a person who is deceitful and cunning.

Eels are very slippery creatures therefore impossible to catch, especially when they are wet. They would just slip right out of your hands.

Example: The company director is **as slippery as an eel**. He should have been put in prison for embezzlement but he manages to hide his tracks so cleverly.

As slow as a snail/as slow as a tortoise

Meaning: Snails and tortoises are well known for their slow pace so we compare a person's slowness to that of a snail or a tortoise.

Example: We will have to find someone else to do the job. Mark is too slow. He is **as slow as a snail**. He likes perfection but there is no room for perfection when we have a deadline to meet.

As sour as vinegar

Meaning: This refers to a person's character more than anything else; someone who displays disagreement or disapproval for almost everything. It is the complete opposite of the similes 'as sweet as sugar', 'as sweet as candy' and 'as sweet as honey'.

Example: I don't really like Sandra. She's **as sour as vinegar**. She is not an easy person to be around.

Her face was **as sour as vinegar** when I told her exactly what I thought of her.

It can also refer to food.

Example: This milk is not fresh. It is **as sour as vinegar**.

Where did you buy these apples? They're **as sour as vinegar**. Take them back to where you got them and get them to change them for some sweeter ones.

To stand as much chance as a snowball in hell

Meaning: This simile is used to refer to a situation which is impossible.

If a snowball is near fire, it melts so it has no chance of survival.

Example: John **stands about as much chance as a snowball in hell** in getting the job. He has no qualifications. (See other examples in 'weather idioms')

As straight as an arrow

Meaning: This refers to an honest and genuine person who can be trusted.

Example: I can trust John blindfolded. He is **as straight as an arrow**.

As strong as an ox

Meaning: Very strong.

Example: That builder, who is working across the road, must be **as strong as an ox**. I saw him carrying a ton of bricks on one shoulder earlier today.

As stubborn as a mule

Meaning: An extremely obstinate person.

Mules are very stubborn animals.

Example: I tried to persuade John to stop drinking, but he is **as stubborn as a mule**. There is no *getting through to him.

As sure as fate

Meaning: This means that it is an absolute certainty that something will happen.

Example: **As sure as fate** she arrived late. (We were certain that this would happen)

Other variations are: as sure as death/as sure as hell.

As sweet as honey/sugar/candy

Meaning: When someone is very sweet, we refer to them using either one of the three similes above.

Example: She **was as sweet as honey/sugar/candy** with me last night. I suspect she wants something from me. This behaviour is very unlike how she normally is. Usually she is normally **as sour as vinegar**.

As thick as thieves

Meaning: Close allies. Since thieves who work together have a close relationship and will always defend one another, we use this simile to describe a bond between two people.

Example: Have you noticed how Sarah and Mary **are as thick as thieves**? Nothing or nobody can come between them.

As thick as two short planks

Meaning: Planks are pieces wood used in the building industry. When we say someone is **as thick as two short planks**, it means they lack intelligence.

As thin as a rake

Meaning: Unhealthily thin. All bones and no flesh.

A rake is a garden tool which looks like a kind of fork. It is used for gathering clutter, old leaves etc.

We can also say 'as skinny as a rake' (all bones and no flesh).

Example: She's **as thin as a rake** since she started that new diet. She'd better be careful she doesn't become anorexic.

As tough as old boots

Meaning: This simile can be used in several contexts.

Example: **She is as tough as old boots**. (She is able to protect herself from anyone or any situation)

This meat is **as tough as old boots**. (Not tender, very difficult to cut and difficult to chew)

My old car is **as tough as old boots**. I've been driving it for years and it has never given me any problems whatsoever.

As ugly as sin

Meaning: Very ugly/disgustingly horrible to look at. This can refer to appearance or a person's character.

Example: She is a very unpleasant person. Every time she speaks she reveals herself to be **as ugly as sin**.

That man is repulsive. In fact he is **as ugly as sin**.

As vast as an ocean

Meaning: This simile is very often used to describe one's love. It describes greatness and enormity.

Example: Boyfriend to girlfriend: I love you so much. My love for you is **as vast as an ocean**.

As warm as toast

Meaning: Usually when we eat toast it is warm so this simile is used to compare anything that is warm as toast.

Example: My house is lovely and warm now that we've had our new heating system installed. It's great to sit on the sofa and watch a movie and feel **as warm as toast**.

As white as a sheet/as white as a ghost

Meaning: Both the above similes are used in the same way.

Extremely pale/when the colour drains from your face.

Example: She was **as white as a ghost/shee**t when I told her the company didn't need her anymore.

As white as snow

Meaning: Very white indeed.

Example: As well as being known for bringing peace, the *dove's beauty lies in its colour. It is **as white as snow**.

*A dove is a bird associated with Easter. It is a symbol of peace and purity.

As wise as an owl

Meaning: To be very wise indeed.

Owls live to a very old age so are considered to become very wise. They have large intelligent looking eyes that stare and *take in everything around them. In fact it looks as if they are wearing large glasses. They cannot move their eyes so when they want to look around them, they have to turn their whole head. If we think a person is very wise, then we compare their wisdom to that of an owl.

<u>Example</u>: John: "I don't know what I'm going to do. I've got a job interview tomorrow and I have no idea how to conduct myself."

Mary: "Speak to my grandfather then. He'll give you a few tips. He's **as wise as an owl**."

During World War II, the United States army used this on a poster with the words;

"Soldier .... be like that old bird!

 Silence means security"

"A wise old bird sat in an oak (tree)

The more he heard, the less he spoke,

The less he spoke, the more he heard ...

PROVERBS

A bad workman always blames his tools

Meaning: A person who has done something badly will try to blame their tools rather than admit they have no skill for the job.

A bird in the hand is worth two in the bush

Meaning: It is better to keep what you have than risk losing it for something better.

Example: I have £10,000. If I invest it to try to double it, I may risk losing all of it. It is safer to keep what you have and not try to risk going after something you are unsure of.

A fool at forty is a fool forever

Meaning: If a person isn't mature by the time they reach the age of 40, then there is no hope of them ever changing.

A fool and his money are easily parted

Meaning: This proverb has the literal meaning. Money does not last long with foolish people. They spend it all very unwisely on stupid things.

A leopard can't change its spots

Meaning: This means that you cannot change a person's character even more so if it is bad.

A stitch in time saves nine

Meaning: This means that if there is a problem that needs to be solved today, then solve it as tomorrow it could be worse and take more time to solve. If there is a hole in your jeans, then you should stitch them now or the hole will be bigger tomorrow therefore *taking up more of your time.

A watched pot never boils

Meaning: If you want to heat water until it boils, and you watch it while you wait, then it seems to take a very long time. In the same way, anything that we wait for with eager attention seems to take a very long time: like waiting for someone to arrive, waiting for the phone to ring, waiting for a letter to come. It is better to distract yourself while waiting.

All's well that ends well

Meaning: An event that has a good ending is good even if some things went wrong along the way. This is the name of a play by Shakespeare. I'm glad you finally got here, even though your car *broke down on the way.

Oh, well. All's well that ends well. The groom was late for the wedding, but everything worked out all right. All's well that ends well.

An apple a day keeps the doctor away

Meaning: If you eat an apple every day, it keeps you in good health.

As you make your bed, so must you lie on it

Meaning: Face the consequences of your wrong actions. You left your wife for another woman, now you realise it was all a mistake. She tells you: 'I don't want you anymore. You have **made your bed and now you must lie on it**.

Barking dogs seldom bite

Meaning: Those who make loud threats seldom *carry them out.

Beauty is in the eye of the beholder

Meaning: What is beautiful for one person may not be beautiful for another. We all see things differently.

Beauty is only skin deep

Meaning: A person's character is more important than their appearance. Beauty is only on the surface of a person. It is what is under that is more important.

Birds of a feather flock together

<u>Meaning</u>: The same types of people attract each other. If you are bad then you will keep bad company. If you are a good person then you will seek the company of people similar to yourself.

Clothes don't make the man

<u>Meaning</u>: Appearances can be deceiving. Similar to 'you can't judge a book by its cover'.

Do not keep all your eggs in the one basket

<u>Meaning</u>: Do not risk everything on the success of one venture. If you invest all your money in one thing, you could lose it all if things go wrong. If you have it invested in different things, then if one goes wrong, you still have the others to *<u>fall back on</u>.

Don't count your chickens before they hatch

<u>Meaning</u>: Making plans on an assumption that is not guaranteed, could lead to disappointment/don't rely on something until you are sure that you have it. If you spend money before you've even earned it, then maybe something will happen and you won't earn this money.

Don't dig your own grave

Meaning: Don't do anything that will cause yourself pain or attract bad things into your life.

Every dog has its day

Meaning: Everyone will get a period of success or satisfaction during his lifetime.

Familiarity breeds contempt

Meaning: When you're around someone for too long and become too familiar with them and their ways, you could get tired of them and annoyed by them and you could even start to dislike them.

Gardens are not made by sitting in the shade

Meaning: Nothing is achieved without effort.

God helps those who help themselves.

Meaning: Success comes to those who make a real effort to achieve it. This has the same meaning as the previous proverb.

Great minds think alike

Meaning: Smart people often have the same ideas.

Half a loaf is better than no bread

Meaning: Be grateful for what you have rather than complaining about what you don't have.

Haste makes waste

Meaning: You should never hurry with a job. If you rush, you will do the job badly therefore requiring much more time and effort to repair the damage. A good architect will spend more time planning and designing. The job will be perfect the first time so there will be no need to go back and start all over again.

If you wish good advice, consult an old man

Meaning: Old people have a lot of experience. If you want to have good advice or recommendations, ask an old person, not a young one.

I'll cross that bridge when I get to it

Meaning: Don't fill your head with thoughts of a possible future problem. This only makes you worry, possibly for no reason when there is no problem at the moment. You cannot cross a bridge if you haven't reached that bridge yet. So when or if the problem arises, then deal with it in that moment. You gain nothing by worrying. You do nothing other than destroy the present moment.

Knowledge is power

<u>Meaning</u>: You should try to learn a lot. Knowing more things makes you more powerful. You can feel stronger.

Kill two birds with one stone

<u>Meaning</u>: Accomplish two different things at the same time.

<u>Example</u>: I took the dog with me to the supermarket because I didn't have enough time to go shopping and take him for a walk as well. That way, I **killed two birds with one stone**.

Kindness begets kindness

<u>Meaning</u>: If you are kind to people, your kindness will be returned.

Lie down with dogs, wake up with fleas

<u>Meaning</u>: If you associate with dishonest people, you will probably *<u>end up</u> like them. Bad things will happen to you as a consequence.

Necessity is the mother of invention

<u>Meaning</u>: The need for something forces people to find a way of obtaining it.

No news is good news

Meaning: If the news was bad, we would hear of it. Since we have heard nothing, we can assume that all is well.

One man's trash is another man's treasure

Meaning: What is valuable for one person may be of no value to another.

Patience is a virtue

Meaning: If you have the ability to wait for something without getting angry or upset then you have a really valuable quality.

Rome was not built in a day

Meaning: It takes time to a job properly. You should not expect to do it quickly.

Speech is silver, silence is golden

Meaning: Speaking is good, but discretion can be better.

Strike while the iron is hot

Meaning: When you have a good opportunity, *go for it. Don't wait for too long to decide. If you have a problem, deal with it when it arises.

Tall oaks from little acorns grow

Meaning: Large successful operations can begin in a small way just as tall oaks start off as small acorns.

Tell me who you go with and I'll tell you who you are

Meaning: Similar to "Birds of a feather...", this proverb suggests that people who think the same tend to always be together. They seem to attract one another like magnets.

The best advice is found on the pillow

Meaning: A good night's sleep may help us find an answer to our problem.

The best things in life are free

Meaning: We don't have to pay for the things that are really valuable, like love, friendship and good health. These thing are there, free of charge.

The truth is in the wine

Meaning: People speak more freely under the influence of alcohol.

The way to a man's heart is through his stomach

Meaning: Many women have won a man's love by cooking delicious meals for him. They fed his stomach and found love in his heart.

There's no time like the present

Meaning: If you need to do something, don't wait until later. Do it now.

Too many cooks spoil the broth

Meaning: Too many people trying to manage something simply spoil it. Everyone is giving orders, but no one is following them! Too many cooks spoil the broth.

Two wrongs don't make a right

Meaning: It is wrong to harm someone because they have harmed you.

Where there's a will there's a way

Meaning: When a person really wants to do something, he will find a way to do it.

You can lead a horse to water but you can't make it drink

Meaning: You can give people good advice but you cannot force them to take this advice.

What goes around comes around

Meaning: If you do bad things to other people, bad things will happen to you and if you do good things to others then good things will happen to.

You cannot judge a book by its cover

Meaning: Do not be deceived by outward appearances. It is what is on the inside that matters the most.

You can't teach an old dog new tricks

Meaning: This means it is difficult to make someone change the way they do something when they have been doing it the same way for a long time

Example: You're never going to be able to teach your father at the age of 75 to use a computer. **You can't teach an old dog new tricks**.

You reap what you sow

Meaning: You will either enjoy or suffer the consequences of your earlier actions or inactions.

PHRASAL VERBS GLOSSARY

The following phrasal verbs appeared throughout the book. Explanations were given according to the context they appeared in. Below is a glossary which explains the different meanings of these phrasal verbs.

Along with

Together with

Ask someone out

Invite someone to go out on a romantic appointment.

Be up to

1) Do

What are you up to on Saturday? What are you doing?

2) Implies devious behaviour -as seen in the following example.

What are the children up to? Can you go and see?

3) Decide

It isn't up to me, it's up to you. This implies that I am not in a position to decide but you are.

Break down

1) Stop functioning for anything electrical, electronic or mechanical

2) When a person becomes emotionally upset he or she breaks down

Break in/to

Force entry into premises with the intention of stealing.

Break up

1) End a relationship

2) Make into smaller pieces

Brighten up

1) Make brighter

2) Make happier

Call (someone) in

Ask a person /professional in the field - to come to your home to do a job

Carry out

Accomplish/execute a plan

Close down

Not be in business anymore/close a business for good (forever)

Come back

Return

Come by

1) Find something by chance

2) Pay a quick visit to someone

Come in/into

1) Enter

2) Come into money = to acquire money from some kind of unexpected source

Come on

1) Make progress

2) Hurry (come on! we're late)

Come over

Be suddenly effected emotionally, so much so that your normal behaviour changes

Come up

Numbers extracted in a game such as the lottery

Come up with

Have the ability to think of an idea or a solution

Count on

Similar to 'rely on' -when you trust that a person will be there for you in moments of need

Crackdown on

Finally stop something that has been going on for quite some time

Crop up

Unexpectedly appear or unexpectedly happen

Eat out

Eat in a restaurant or café or such like

End up

In the end after considering different options this happens or this is done

Fall back on

To have something you to use in case of an emergency

Fall for (something)

Believe something untrue that someone tells you. Usually when you 'fall for something that someone tells you', it implies that you are a gullible person.

Fall for (someone)

Be really attracted to a person

Fall into

Be within a range of parameters

Fall off (something)

Used when you are on something such as a chair, a bike, a motorbike etc. and you fall from it onto the floor or ground.

Fed up with (someone or something)

To be tired of this thing or person

Fell off

Fall from a height to the floor or to the ground.

Find out

Discover or be informed.

Be fond of (someone or something)

Like something a lot. When used with 'someone' it means feel affection for that person

Gamble away

Waste all your money by gambling. When you gamble you place bets such as on the horses or football pools or the lottery. scratch cards, roulette and slot machines and suchlike.

Get on

Board a bus, train or other vehicle which involves moving your feet upward to board'

Get on with (someone)

Have a good relationship

Get through to (someone)

1) Make a person understand -usually they do not want to understand

2) On the phone: Be able to connect the line to someone

Get up

Leave your bed/move up from a sitting position.

Give back

Return something you borrowed

Give up

Stop doing (something)/renounce

Give way

Collapse

Go bust

Go out of business/go bankrupt -go into financial ruin

Go for it

Grab the opportunity

Go on

Progress/continue/happening

Go on (verb collocation) collocated with:

Go on holiday/go on a cruise/go on a picnic/ go on a trip/go on a business trip/go on a retreat/go on a pilgrimage

Go out

Leave the house to go somewhere

Go out with (someone)

Frequent a person as a boyfriend or girlfriend.

Go through

Experience something (usually unpleasant).

Go through with something

Go ahead and do something unpleasant that you have no desire to do but you have to do it against your will.

Go through/be through

Experience something

Go under

Sink like a ship when you go bankrupt. Your business has failed

Go up

Increase

Grow up

Grow from a child to an adult'. This phrasal verb can only be used for people

Hand in

Give -normally to someone in authority such as a teacher or a policeman. You can 'hand in' money if you find any, to the police station

Head off

Begin to go somewhere/start a journey -even a short one from your home to the end of the street

Hurry up

Be quick

Leave (someone) alone

Leave in peace/not bother/annoy a person

Lie down

Put yourself in a horizontal position on a surface such as a bed or sofa -usually because you want to rest or sleep

Look after

The same as take care of -tend to something or someone to make sure it has what it needs

Mount up

Accumulate

Move out

Stop living in one place and go to live in another

Pay back

Give back money you borrowed

Pay (something) off

Completely pay everything you owe

Put (something) off

Postpone/move to a later date

Put on weight

Gain weight/become fatter

Put up with

Tolerate

Rip (someone) off

Swindle a person

Run away

Escape

Run up

Accumulate debt

Settle down

1) Get married/stop being single and live a regular life

2) Become calm

Snap at someone

Give a quick angry reply

Switch on

Put something electrical or electronic into operation

Take in

Absorb with the mind

Take on

Commit oneself to a task

Take up

Occupy time or space

Think something through

Carefully think before deciding

Trick someone into something

Obtain something from someone deceptively by misleading the person into thinking that you have good honest intentions

Turn (sound) down

Lower the volume

Turn down

Not accept/refuse

Turn out

Reveal (to be)

Turn up

Appear

Wake up

Finish sleeping

Watch out for someone or something

Be attentive in order not to miss someone or something.

Watch over

Guard and protect by keeping your eyes on the person or thing. (A mother dog watches over her puppies)

Work out

Understand

Made in the USA
San Bernardino, CA
09 November 2018